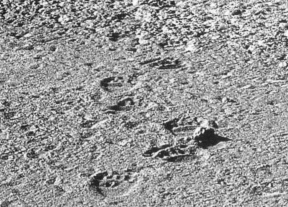

Backcountry Bear Basics

**The Definitive
Guide to
Avoiding
Unpleasant
Encounters**

SECOND EDITION

Dave Smith

THE MOUNTAINEERS BOOKS

This book is dedicated to my parents, who let me run wild in the woods while the other kids were stuck in Sunday school.

THE MOUNTAINEERS BOOKS
*is the nonprofit publishing arm of The Mountaineers Club,
an organization founded in 1906 and dedicated to the exploration,
preservation, and enjoyment of outdoor and wilderness areas.*

1001 SW Klickitat Way, Suite 201, Seattle, WA 98134

© 2006 by Dave Smith

First printing 1997, second printing 1998, third printing 2004. Second edition, 2006.

Published simultaneously in Great Britain by Cordee, 3a DeMontfort Street, Leicester, England, LE1 7HD

Manufactured in the United States of America

Project Editor: Susan Hodges
Copyeditor: Susan Hodges
Cover and Book Design: Karen Schober Book Design
Layout: Marge Mueller, Gray Mouse Graphics
Cover photograph: *Brown bear* © Ferenc Cegled, Shutterstock, Inc.
Frontispiece: *Grizzly tracks*

A *Cataloging-in-Publication record is on file at the Library of Congress.*

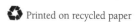 Printed on recycled paper

Contents

Acknowledgments

It seems like Doug Peacock and I have spent more time talking about what to cook for dinner than the food habits of bears; nevertheless, his respect for the rights of grizzlies has had an enormous influence on my thoughts about the great bear.

I spend an inordinate amount of time dwelling on bears, so it's been a pleasure discussing bears with many of the biologists and experts listed below. Their passion is inspiring. My thanks for reviewing the manuscript go to Larry Aumiller (Alaska Department of Fish and Game), Tom Beck (retired, Colorado Division of Wildlife); Steve French (Yellowstone Grizzly Foundation); Kerry Gunther (Yellowstone National Park); Polly Hessing, Colleen Matt (Alaska Department of Fish and Game); Rick McAdam (Yellowstone National Park); Lewis Sharman (Glacier Bay National Park); and Derek Stonorov (Alaska Department of Fish and Game). I'm also grateful to Mike Swain and Ed Vorisek (Denali National Park) and Lisa Peacock for reviewing portions of the manuscript.

In phone conversations and correspondence, Steve French and Tom Beck were generous with their time and their understanding of bears. Talking bears with Alaska Department of Fish and Game biologist John Hechtel is always enlightening. Steve Herrero has been a great source for accurate, scientific data on bear attacks. Brighan Young University (BYU) professor Tom Smith's advice and encouragement have been invaluable.

There's no way I can express my gratitude to the McNeil River crew—Larry Aumiller, Polly Hessing, Colleen Matt, and Derek Stonorov—for sharing their knowledge of bears with me. Colleen in particular helped shape the book with her gentle insistence on finding ways to reach people with accurate facts about bears.

Sleepy bears yawn, but during an encounter with another bear or a person, yawning is a sign of anxiety. Bear behavior can be complex.

Others who helped along the way include Larry Campbell (Friends of the Bitterroot); Jasper Carlton (Biodiversity Legal Foundation); Hod Coburn, Mitch Friedman (Greater Ecosystem Alliance); Jim McBride, Keith Hammer (Swan View Coalition); Ken Leghorn, Jim Peaco (Yellowstone); Lynn Rogers, Roger Rudolph, John Scheerens, Tom Walker, and Louisa Willcox.

If I've left anyone out, my apologies. If there are any factual errors in this book, they're mine and mine alone.

NO GUARANTEES IN BEAR COUNTRY

There are no guarantees in bear country. Bears kill an average of three people a year in North America, and injure more. Following the recommendations in this book will reduce your risk of encountering a bear. You'll learn the best techniques for deterring a bear and minimizing injuries in the event of an attack. I've consulted with numerous bear experts and wildlife agencies to insure the accuracy of this book. Nevertheless, interactions between bears and humans are incredibly complex, and I assume no liability for injuries or death by bears.

Introduction

The bears of remote areas, unaccustomed to human traffic, may be more timid than average.
　　　　　　—John Hart, *Walking Softly in the Wilderness: The Sierra Club Guide to Backpacking,* 1983

It is mainly wild black bears found in rural or remote areas—where they have relatively little association with people—that occasionally try to kill and eat a human being.
　　　　　　—Stephen Herrero, *Bear Attacks: Their Causes and Avoidance,* 1985

Bear literature is confusing and contradictory. Inaccurate assumptions masquerade as biological axioms, and conventional wisdom about bears is often just bad advice. The same books and brochures that advise you to climb a tree to safety to escape a charging grizzly insist that you should never run from a bear. They tell you not to run because flight can trigger pursuit and you won't win a race with a bear; they say climb a tree instead, because adult grizzlies can't. Whoa. Hold on. Before you start climbing, ask yourself two critical questions. First, if flight is likely to trigger pursuit, won't grizzlies chase tree-climbers and track stars with equal abandon? Second, how much time will you have to squirrel up a tree when you startle a grizzly at 60 yards or less? Conventional wisdom may say climb a tree to safety, but knowing that a bear can outrun you tells you that sprinting for and then trying to climb a tree after a bear begins its charge is a dangerous mistake—you won't have time.

What about the widespread belief that bears have poor vision? Is it true, or is it a myth based on the tall tales of mountain men? This is not an academic question when you spot a female grizzly with two cubs 80 yards away. Let's say the bears are not aware of your presence. A steady 12-mile-per-hour wind is blowing in your face. The bears aren't going to smell you, and they won't hear you if you keep quiet. So can they see you standing there? Will they spot you if you move? You need to know because their visual acuity dictates your next move.

Backcountry Bear Basics will separate facts from fallacies and give you detailed information on how to travel and camp safely in bear country. The emphasis will be on preventing unpleasant incidents; first choose a good campsite and properly store your food, and then worry about whether or not pepper spray will protect you from a bear investigating your camp.

Don't count on pepper spray to get you out of trouble. Instead, take common-sense precautions to avoid putting yourself in a situation where you need to use it.

I try to allow the natural behavior and habits of bears to guide my conduct when I'm afield. Statistics prove that hiking with two or more people significantly reduces the likelihood of a bear attack. One, more people tend to make more noise—you're less likely to startle a bear at close range. Two, if you do startle a nearby bear and it charges, it's far more likely to make contact with a solo hiker than with two or more people who stick close together. I prefer the risks (and rewards) of traveling alone to the guilt I feel for hiking with a noisy mob of people that displaces bears from their preferred habitat. Although I clap my hands or call out loudly when I'm in thick cover, I don't go to extremes like blasting portable boat horns. We can't ignore the fact that even non-lethal methods of enhancing human safety in bear country can be detrimental to bears, especially our beleaguered grizzlies in the Lower

48 states. In *Backcountry Bear Basics,* I'll explain your options, describe the consequences of your actions on bears, and let your conscience be your guide.

FACT OR FALLACY

Never get between a sow and her cubs, bears eat anything and everything, never make eye contact with a bear…you've probably heard these truisms before. Are they true, false, or a half-bubble off level? Scattered throughout *Backcountry Bear Basics,* you'll find Fact or Fallacy sidebars that provide accurate, up-to-date information on common beliefs about bears.

> "I have tried to solve the riddle of why so many popular beliefs are erroneous. The best answer that I have been able to evolve, so far, is that someone starts a rumor, which is false. The next person who hears this rumor remarks: 'You cannot believe all you

If you see grizzly cubs, assume their protective mother is nearby.

hear,' but nevertheless repeats it, and by constant repetition it merges into: 'Everybody says so.' When everybody says so, it becomes an acknowledged fact and popular belief is thus born. After this, if anyone ventures to assail its truth, he is likely to be looked at and considered 'queer.'"

—Montague Stevens, *Meet Mr. Grizzly,* 1944

Hikers and hunters agree that bears are exceptionally intelligent creatures, yet the February 1995 cover of *Backpacker* magazine featured an article titled "The Real Truth about Grizzlies: Why You Have Little to Fear," while that same month the cover of *Outdoor Life* magazine had a piece titled "Should We Hunt Grizzlies: A Tale of Terror Holds the Answer." Why would an intelligent animal flee from unarmed hikers, yet charge hunters toting a .375 H&H Magnum rifle capable of dropping an elephant? This suicidal behavior suggests that either bears are stupid or people twist facts to make bears into whatever we want them to be. Bears aren't stupid. Nor are grizzly bears territorial, but it's a lot easier to say "grizzlies attack humans to defend their territory" than it is to look for the real reasons why bears injure people. From the modern myth that menstruating women should stay out of bear country to the old misconception that bears have difficulty running downhill, bear literature is rife with erroneous information and self-serving facts.

Pejorative language limits our knowledge of bears. In *Yosemite: The Embattled Wilderness,* historian Alfred Runte notes that even well-meaning bear advocates use terms like "marauding," "offending," and "troublesome" to describe the very bears they're dedicated to protecting.[1] You won't encounter any "problem bears" in *Backcountry Bear Basics,* and we're going to examine the veracity of clichés about "unpredictable bears" making "bluff charges." Clichés and pejorative language act as blinders that keep you from seeing bears for what they really are.

Sound information about bears is vital because what you don't know about bears can endanger you. Consider the following excerpt from an article in *Field & Stream,* which was accompanied by a picture of a bear down on all fours directly facing the photographer who wrote the story:

> Every few minutes, the sow grizzly raised her head and stared at me. Satisfied that I posed no threat, she continued to devour red soap berries from the brushy Alaskan slope. The sow probably weighed 350 pounds, but at 70 feet, she appeared much larger...I watched intently for any indication that she was unhappy with my presence in her territory, but there was none. The hair on her neck was

not raised in alarm, and she made no noise other than the guttural sounds that come from a bear gathering a berry breakfast... Suddenly, without warning, she charged![2]

"I've never seen a bear raise its hackles," said Terry DeBruyn during an Alaska Interagency Bear Safety Education Committee (AIBSEC) meeting in 2000. The sound people expect to hear from a bear is a growl, but it's uncommon for grizzlies to growl. And biologist Lynn Rogers writes, "Growls are rare or absent in black bears."[3] Evidently,

If you're engaged in a close-up encounter with a bear and it yawns, the bear is not bored. Yawning is a sign of low-level stress.

the author expected warnings that bears don't give. Any wild animal that frequently stops feeding or other activities to watch you is a bit uneasy. Whether you're watching bears or porcupines, you have an ethical obligation to stop bothering the animal, and it's just plain stupid to keep pressing a grizzly bear that's only 70 feet away. During an encounter between two bears, frontal orientation—facing directly toward an antagonist—can signify dominance or a willingness to attack. In other words, the bear in our story expressed its anxiety with a person who was way too close, but the photographer didn't recognize the signs. Ignorance is not bliss in bear country, and if you go afield with preconceptions about bears that are misconceptions, your false assumptions could prove costly.

Brown bears in the Pyrenees Mountains of Spain are the same species as North America's fabled grizzlies, yet centuries of human domination and selective killing that eliminates the boldest bears have turned them into ghosts that are rarely seen. Illegal hunting, incremental habitat loss, and incessant harassment by everyone from mountain bikers to bubbleheads on snowmobiles might turn Yellowstone's grizzlies into ghost bears. They may adapt and survive, but their haunting presence would only serve as a reminder of all that's been lost. Instead of Ursus arctos horriblis, we'll have Ursus arctos emasculatis. I refuse to accept that, so my goal for writing *Backcountry Bear Basics* goes beyond giving tips to make your trip to bear country safer; I want to make the world a better place for bears. Fortunately, these two objectives go hand in hand. I'm convinced that if we can accommodate bears in our world, it will be a better place for us to live, too.

chapter
1

Planning a Trip into Bear Country

As with most safety issues, proper preparation for bear country camping begins before the trip.
—Ken Leghorn, Sea Kayaker magazine, 1987

Planning for a trip into bear country involves learning a bit about bears and the area you intend to visit, packing essential equipment, and making sure you have the proper attitude—you accept the risks of traveling in bear country and accept responsibility for the consequences of your actions.

RESEARCH

Always get general information on bear activity in the area you plan to visit well in advance of your trip, and then get up-to-date facts when you arrive. Many parks and forests closely monitor bear activity, and they will be happy to pass on information.

If you're planning months in advance for a trip to Kluane National Park in the Yukon, call or write for basic information and check on the feasibility of your plans. Sometimes people study topographic maps and trail guides and make up their mind they're going to hike to Eagle Peak the first week of September, no matter what. When they arrive in Kluane, they discover the Eagle Peak area is closed because several grizzly bears have gathered there to feast on huckleberries. There's a temptation to hike in anyhow. So what if it's dangerous? Who cares if you drive away a few bears? You've been thinking about this trip for six months.

If you had called in advance, somebody could have told you the Eagle Peak area has been closed in September for the past three years. Resource management experts can often predict when and where to expect bears because the bruins are so keyed in to seasonal food sources. As biologist Terry DeBruyn mentions in *Walking with Bears,* "[t]he most important element dictating when and where bears are likely to be found is food availability. This is especially true in fall." You might save yourself from disappointment or disaster by contacting land managers well in advance of your trip and asking for their recommendations.

Once you arrive at your destination, even if you're not required to check in and get a permit before setting off on a hike or canoe trip, it's still a good idea to get up-to-date information on the places you plan to visit. You don't want to camp at a site that a bear raided the night before. Also, check the signs at trailheads for up-to-the-minute notices.

Part of your advance planning should include researching bears themselves and how they interact with humans. There are several good books and videos available about bears (see "Recommended References"). In particular, I recommend the International Association for Bear Research and Management's (IBA) *Staying Safe in Bear Country* video. You get to hear the "jaw popping" sound a bear makes when it is nervous and see the incredible speed of a charging bear. You get to watch the bear behavior you need to understand to be well prepared for an excursion into bear country. Just as importantly, you will have less fear of bears, which is often just a fear of the unknown.

What if there's a black bear in your camp at night? What if a grizzly bear charges you? It's important to know how you should—or shouldn't—respond to bears during close encounters. You have to focus on bears before you go afield, not after you've hiked 2 miles. People have been injured or killed by bears "just a half-mile from the trailhead." For example, three people were injured by grizzlies near the Eagle River Nature Center in Alaska's Chugach State Park during the 1990s.[2] Don't make the mistake of thinking the bears are "out there" and you're safe near human artifacts on the edge of wildlands. Be knowledgeable and alert the instant you enter the woods.

BEAR ESSENTIALS

Don't forget special bear paraphernalia as you pack for your trip. If you're the type of person who uses a camping equipment checklist, put the "bear gear" you plan on using at the top of the list:

- A bear-resistant food container (see "Cooking and Food Storage")
- Resealable plastic bags and garbage bags ("Cooking and Food Storage")
- Fifty to 100 feet of cord or rope and two stuff sacks for hanging food, if you use the counterbalance method ("Cooking and Food Storage")
- Binoculars ("Camping and Travel Tips")
- A tent ("Camping and Travel Tips")
- A flashlight ("Camping and Travel Tips")
- Pepper spray ("Guns and Pepper Spray")
- A sheath knife with a 3- to 5-inch blade or a folding knife with a locking blade
- A portable electric fence

Some people tote firearms in places where it's legal, but you should carefully consider the information in "Guns and Pepper Spray" before packing a firearm.

SLEEP WELL: ELECTRIC FENCES

When BYU professor Tom Smith first began working in Katmai National Park, there were so many bears in camp at night that his research on bear behavior turned into "a study on human 'sleep deprivation.'"[3]

The solution to this problem? Portable electric fences. The National Outdoor Leadership School (NOLS) uses portable electric fences. They work. Several companies now sell portable electric fences, and while most are too heavy and bulky for a solo backpacker, they're manageable for canoeists in Minnesota's Boundary Waters. The weight and bulk wouldn't matter if you were car camping at a primitive U.S. Forest Service campground in bear country at the end of a dirt road. The lightweight champ at the moment is a two pound fence that encloses a 20' X 20' area.

A variety of electric fences is available from High Country Enterprise, www.electorbearguard.com. You can find a plan to build your own electric fence at the U.S. Geological Survey website for Alaska, www.absc.usgs.gov/research/brownbears/safety/electric_fencing.htm.

BEWARE OF SENSATIONALISM

> "In popular literature, films, and television, bears have been demonized or humanized."
>
> —*Staying Safe in Bear Country* video, International Association for
> Bear Research and Management

I think it's difficult for people to have realistic expectations about bears because bears are routinely portrayed in an extreme manner. They're either Disneyland characters or a land-dwelling version of the monstrous shark in *Jaws*.

The late Timothy Treadwell represents the Disneyland extreme. On *The Late Show with David Letterman,* Treadwell said grizzly bears were mostly "party animals." On Discovery Channel's *Grizzly Diaries,* Treadwell sang to bears, blew them kisses, and told them "I love you." In his book *Among Grizzlies,* Treadwell gave bears names like Cupcake and Thumper. For 13 years—until the day Timothy and his companion were killed and eaten by a bear—Treadwell showed us how incredibly tolerant coastal brown bears can be. That's one side of bears. Treadwell gave us a one-dimensional view of bears, not a complete portrait. I believe part of Treadwell's motivation for showing us the tolerant side of grizzly bears was to prove that bears are not the monsters you meet in "hook-and-bullet" magazines such as *Field & Stream* or *North American Hunter*.

When *Outdoor Life* celebrated its 100th anniversary, one editor wrote an essay about the venerable magazine's tradition of publishing gruesome bear attack tales: "Our writers scoured the country for the most horrific mauling stories—the office code for these tales was 'scalp flappers'—and readers never got tired of them."[4] One hundred years of "scalp flappers" has created a fear of bears all out of proportion to the actual risk and made generations of hunters trigger-happy. The tradition continues. In 2005, *North American Hunter* published an article on black bear hunting titled "Nightmare Bear," complete with a tale about "A Diabolical Bear," a "500-pound bruin" that "could have torn my legs off!"[5] Hyperbole is the "hook-and-bullet" magazines' stock-in trade. In these publications, hunters rarely encounter a small or average-sized bear that flees the instant it detects them; instead, it's a big bear glaring balefully at the hunters before the bruin attacks "without warning."

> We have, as one writer put it, 'demonized' the bear through popular writings, scary stories, and barroom hunting yarns. We seem to need our ghost stories. For every balanced bear book like Thomas

Many unscrupulous photographers, writers, and publishers don't tell you their scary pictures of bears are digitally altered photos, trained bears, or bears in animal farms. This ranger is being "attacked" by a stuffed bear.

McNamee's *The Grizzly Bear*, a dozen others, like *Alaska Bear Tales*, only harm the image of bears through lopsided and often unsubstantiated reporting.

—Tom Walker, *River of Bears*

Magazines like *Outdoor Life* have nothing on books like *Mark of the Grizzly*, *Alaska Bear Tales*, and *Bear Attacks: The Deadly Truth*, to name a few. These books are so over the top I refer to them as the "Killer Bear Mauls Elvis" genre. "Killer Bear Mauls Elvis" books are filled with sensationalistic bear attack tales that repeat the same basic story again and again. Man meets bear. Bear injures or kills man. Clinical descriptions of the injuries: "The first bite broke Bagley's jaw. The second crushed his cheekbones and separated the row of upper teeth from the rest of his head. One of the bear's canine teeth gouged a hole behind his right eye socket."[6]

Some books even include close-up photos of gaping wounds, claiming that "if looked at objectively with the intent of learning from them, they can help us understand bears."[7]

Sure. Those photos help you understand bears as much as the babes in bikinis on the cover of auto magazines help you understand how to change the oil in your Jeep.

I regard these books as "bear pornography" because if you eliminated the blood and guts—the equivalent of nude women in *Playboy*—nobody would buy them. It's worth noting the women in *Playboy* choose to pose nude, and get paid to strip. The bears in "bear pornography" just get exploited.

The authors of sensationalistic bear books always mention that most bears want nothing to do with people, but after reading nothing but stories about bear attacks, most people conclude that any bear they encounter will attack them. The gruesome stories in "Killer Bear Kills Elvis" books create an unhealthy and unwarranted fear and paranoia about bears.

Maine's hunting guides shamelessly played on these fears when voters were presented with a ballot initiative that would have banned hunting bears with bait, and hunting bears with dogs. The Maine Professional Guide's Association website posted news articles about bear attacks—the unspoken threat was, if you don't let us continue bear hunting in the manner we're accustomed to, bear attacks will increase. The headline for the first story was: "Bear Mauls and Kills Infant in New York State."

If you're fishing in New York's Catskill Park, do you need to worry that every bear in the woods wants to kill and eat you? No. If you're kayaking in Alaska's Glacier Bay National Park and you spot a brown bear along the shore, is it safe to pull ashore, tell ol' Buster the Bear you love him, and then sing him a few verses from Louis Armstrong's "What a Wonderful World?" No. If you do, you might not be long for this world.

YELLOWSTONE NATIONAL PARK BEAR-RELATED INJURIES AND FATALITIES 1992–2001
Backcountry vs. Developed Areas

Year	Total Park Visitors	Backcountry Use Nights (a)	Backcountry Injuries: Grizzly Bear	Backcountry Injuries: Black Bear	Developed Area Injuries: Black or Grizzly
2001	2,752,346	43,302	0	0	0
2000	2,838,233	39,469	2	1	0
1999	3,131,381	43,540	2	0	0
1998	3,120,830	45,612	1	0	0
1997	2,889,513	44,836	1	1	0
1996	3,012,171	45,743	0	0	0
1995	3,125,285	45,774	0	0	0
1994	3,046,645	45,460	4	0	0
1993	2,912,193	45,135	0	0	0
1992	3,186,190	42,124	1	0	0
10 year totals					
	30,014,787	440,995	11	2	0

(a) Backcountry day use records are not collected. Includes overnight backcountry use only.

Backcountry hikers in national parks with grizzlies are far more likely to suffer serious injuries from bears than people who drive through a park and just stop at roadside attractions like Yellowstone's Old Faithful.

Respect bears. Respect the potential bears have to harm people. According to the IBA, "[e]ach year, on average, three people are killed in bear attacks in North America. More are seriously injured."[8] Follow a few commonsense precautions, and you can greatly reduce the risk of being killed or injured by a bear. Bears are not demons. Bears are not Disneyland characters; they're not people dressed in fur suits. Beware of media hype that portrays bears at one extreme or the other.[9]

PRECAUTIONS WITH CHILDREN

Discuss bears with your kids before you go. A study on fatal injuries inflicted by black bears presented at the Fifth Western Black Bear Workshop in 1995 shows that out of thirty-seven documented cases of black bears killing people, five cases involved children ten years and under and another five cases involved people between the ages of ten and nineteen.[10] I don't think we can say that black bears target children as prey because of their small size; however, I do believe it's prudent to try to make your kids understand that bears can be dangerous. Have a talk with your children before going afield, but keep it simple:

1. Never let the adult(s) you're with out of sight.
2. Don't approach bears or other wildlife.
3. Never run from a bear.
4. If you see a bear, don't scream.
5. Stay calm and call loudly for help when you see a bear.

Remember, though, that despite your forceful little speech, kids always seem to wander off and disappear. It's up to you to keep close tabs on your children. When hiking, always keep kids between adults, not at the front or rear of your group.

When hiking with children in bear (or cougar) country, sandwich kids in the middle of your group. Keep adults at the front and rear.

BEAR ATTACKS DEMYSTIFIED

Most "bear attacks" fit into two broad categories. First, black bears and grizzly bears have been known to prey on people. A rare event, but it happens. Since 1900, there have been about twenty cases of black bears preying on people, and half as many predatory incidents involving grizzlies. What flips the switch that causes a bear to prey on a person? Nobody knows. Age, illness, and infirmity are seldom factors.[11]

Second, bears defend themselves from people who encroach on their personal space, the distance that, if entered, forces the bruin to make a decision: fight or flee? You understand the concept of personal space if you've ever been at a party and found yourself kind of leaning away from a stranger who stands a little too close when he's talking with you. The reason you feel uncomfortable is that the guy is in your personal space. While it's accurate to say bears will "fight or flee" when you encroach on their personal space, the term "fight or flee" is a tad dramatic for a typical bear–human encounter. Most of the time, bears detect people before we're aware of them and walk away.

The amount of personal space a bear requires varies. A male grizzly in Denali National Park might ordinarily require 130 yards of personal space. If the same bear is feeding on a caribou carcass, it might need more personal space—say, 190 yards. A solitary female black bear in Banff National Park might remain undisturbed at a distance of 60 yards. A year later when the same bear has cubs at her side, she might go into "fight or flee" mode when you're 110 yards away.

The presence of cubs or a carcass usually increases a bear's personal space requirement. It also increases the likelihood the bear will elect to "fight" if you encroach on its personal space. Most literature stresses that bears defend cubs or carcasses; the following story from Mark of the Grizzly illustrates why I put more emphasis on bears defending their personal space.

In a chapter of the book titled "Warm Spell," an elk-hunting guide and his client near Yellowstone startled a grizzly with cubs, and the bears were only about 30–35 yards away. The sow charged and injured both hunters. The bear charged because the hunters encroached on her personal space, right? Not according to Mark of the Grizzly author Scott McMillion. He says, "The cause of the attack remains unknown. The hunters never came between her and the cubs, and the immediate area contained no gut piles or other food sources she was trying to protect."[12]

You don't have to get between a sow and her cubs to encroach on her personal space and provoke a charge; you just have to get close enough. Cubs or no cubs, carcass or no carcass, at a distance of 30 to 35 yards, you're well within the personal space of a typical Yellowstone grizzly.

Black bears generally flee when you encroach on their personal space. Grizzlies are more likely than black bears to fight in response to an incursion on their personal space, but to put this in perspective, Larry Aumiller estimates that grizzlies flee at least 90 percent of the time when people encroach on their personal space.[13] Even when grizzlies charge, bears often stop short of making contact. Given that you're not likely to know the personal space required by an individual bear, common sense dictates that you give all bears a wide berth. The closer you are to a grizzly when the bear becomes aware of you, the greater the likelihood it will charge. Sudden encounters at close range also increase the likelihood the charging bear will make contact.

There's an invisible boundary line around every bear, and when you cross that line and enter the bear's personal space, you force it to fight or flee.

RESPONSIBILITY

One final note of caution about bear country: The government is not responsible for your safety in bear country—you are. As a general rule, you can get accurate information from rangers and agency personnel about such things as high- and low-density bear areas and locations where bears have been seen recently, but agency folks cannot guarantee your safety in bear country. Just because there weren't any bears on the Whitebark Pine Trail for the past three weeks does not mean you won't bump into one today. All the agencies can do is give you their best educated guess about a complex situation that any bear can change anytime it wants. Again—there's no guarantee of your safety in bear country. If you're injured by a bear, don't blame anyone but yourself. If you're not willing to accept responsibility for your decision to go afield in bear country, go somewhere else.

You don't have to get between a sow and her cubs to encroach on her personal space and provoke a charge.

chapter
2

Bear Evolution, Biology, and Behavior

Beyond a general knowledge of bear biology, such as the physical differences between grizzlies and black bears, it's helpful to know a little about the evolution of bears to understand why they behave the way they do. It's wise to be familiar with the basics of bear behavior so you don't think a nearby bear that yawns at you is bored when in fact it's a bit stressed. Understanding how bears interact with other bears is the key to understanding how bears interact with humans and, in turn, to making the correct moves when you have a close encounter with a bear. This chapter will emphasize the aspects of bear biology, behavior, and evolution that count for backcountry users.

EVOLUTION

Because black bears and grizzly bears walked along different evolutionary paths, the two species often have a different response to what biologists call the "fight or flight" question: How do you respond to a threatening situation? Do you fight, or do you take flight?

Black bears are creatures of the forest, so in response to a threat they've always had the option of slipping into the underbrush and hiding or climbing a tree. When threatened, black bears flee. Even when black bear biologists hold squalling cubs while the mama bear is just yards away, the females almost always retreat. They may make a blowing sound and clack their teeth and make a rush or two toward the biologists but, ultimately, they retreat.

FACT OR FALLACY ?

FALLACY:
Never run from a bear.

FACT:
It's almost always a mistake to run from a bear. However, biologist Terry DeBruyn has written, "There are instances when it is okay to retreat rapidly from a bear: e.g., (if) a cub is on a beach and the mother is upwind and unaware of your presence. A person in this situation would run to distance themselves from a potentially negative encounter."[1]

In an article about bear myths titled "The Bear that Never Was," biologists Steven C. Amstrup, Stephen Herrero, and Tom S. Smith note that "[i]f running allows you to quickly attain safe haven such as a nearby cabin, vehicle, or some other structure—then run."[2] Just don't underestimate a bear's speed and quickness, or overestimate yours.

Not so with grizzlies. Grizzlies evolved in more open terrain. At times, there wasn't enough cover for a female and her cubs to hide from other bears or mammals. There were no trees to climb. When threatened, a female had to defend her cubs.[3] The key word here is *defend*. Grizzlies aren't malicious beasts that lurk in the woods waiting to waylay backpackers. A grizzly may defend itself if it perceives you as a threat, but if you don't bother a grizzly, it will rarely bother you. Granted, this understanding is no comfort to a person who accidentally startles a grizzly at close range and gets injured. Grizzlies do occasionally prey on people; they are not harmless teddy bears. In evolutionary terms, it's perfectly natural for grizzlies to defend themselves. It's an instinctive reaction based on thousands of years of evolutionary history.

One of the most common explanations for bear attacks is that the bear was "defending its territory." As the *Staying Safe in Bear Country* video explains, bears have "... home ranges not territories. Most bears are not territorial and don't try to exclude other bears from the area where they live. Home ranges of individuals typically overlap those of their neighbors."[4]

When people say bears are territorial, they probably mean that a bear might take offense if you encroach on its personal space. Once you're within a bear's personal space and have "engaged" the bruin, it will feel compelled to do something. It might come closer to identify you or better assess the situation, but, ultimately, you've forced it into a situation where it can only flee or attack.

BIOLOGY

Although dozens of books provide in-depth coverage of bear biology, I'm going to shift the normal focus a little to meet the needs of active outdoors people. The fact that a bear's heartbeat drops by around 80 percent during hibernation is irrelevant to cross-country skiers; however, the fact that a few grizzlies in Yellowstone emerge from their dens in March does have significance for folks on skinny skis—you could bump into a bear at the end of a long, downhill run.

Bear Species

Black bears (Ursus americanus) and brown bears (Ursus arctos) are different species. Kodiak bears (Ursus arctos middendorffi) have not been genetically isolated on Alaska's Kodiak Island for long enough to be considered a subspecies of the brown bear. They have the same genetic makeup as brown bears along Alaska's coast.[5] Taxonomists list brown bears and grizzly bears as the same species. People generally call Ursus arctos along the coast of Alaska "brown bears" and Ursus arctos everywhere else "grizzly bears," a convention I follow throughout this book.

Black bears have a straight "roman" facial profile, as opposed to the "dished" profile of a grizzly. The high point on a black bear is its rump.

GRIZZLY AND BLACK BEAR COMPARED

GRIZZLY BEAR	BLACK BEAR
Dished/concave facial profile from tip of nose to top of forehead.	Straight line (Roman) facial profile from tip of nose to forehead.
Relatively small, short, rounded ears.	Larger, more erect, pointed ears, especially on cubs and immature bears.
In spring and fall, mature animals may have ruff of hair under chin.	No ruff of hair under chin.
Hump over front shoulder.	No hump over shoulder—but some body postures give appearance of hump.
Shoulder hump is highest point on body.	Back is highest point on body
Front claws usually at least 1¾ inches long, fairly straight, and light-colored.	Front claws rarely exceed 1½ inches, dark colored, and often sharply curved for climbing.
Track of hind foot has pointed heel.	Track of hind foot has rounded heel.
Straight line drawn across top of main pad of front foot track won't cross toepads.	Straight line drawn across top of main pad of front foot track will cross toepads.
Adults often have grizzled (gray-tipped) cape of long hair over shoulders.	Not grizzled, although they can appear to have a grizzled coat in certain light conditions.

GRIZZLY BEAR

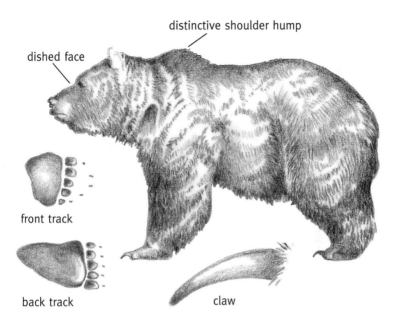

distinctive shoulder hump

dished face

front track

back track

claw

BLACK BEAR

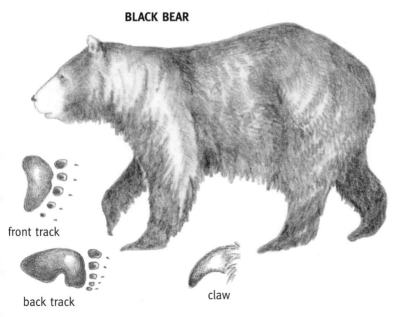

front track

back track

claw

Even bear experts can have trouble distinguishing black bears from grizzlies in the field because the key physical differences listed below are not always readily apparent.

BLACK BEARS ARE NOT MINI-GRIZZLIES

In *Walking with Bears,* (p.76) biologist Terry DeBruyn tells an enlightening story about the tendency of black bears to flee rather than fight when a person suddenly encroaches on their personal space. DeBruyn needed to determine cub survival rates for a study area, so he used telemetry equipment to help him sneak up on radio-collared females with cubs. Keep in mind that DeBruyn is a skilled outdoorsman. In addition to knowing where the bears were because of the telemetry equipment, he tried to move in on the bears when the wind was in his face and environmental conditions were optimal. "On twenty-seven of fifty-two attempts at sneaking in, the bear families detected my approach and fled before I was able to make visual contact. On the other occasions, I was able to approach the families to within 50 yards and then rush them, sending the cubs up nearby refuge trees so I could count them. Although I surprised the females and their cubs at very close range, on every one of those occasions, the females abandoned their cubs and fled the area."[6]

This is not a technique any biologist would use to count grizzly bear cubs—at least not for long. It does illustrate a point biologist Tom Beck made to me years ago—black bears are not mini-grizzlies. Behaviorally, they're a different animal.

You should still keep your distance from black bears, especially females with cubs. But the risk of bumping into a black bear on the trail and have it respond by charging you is vastly overrated.

Male or Female?

Males urinate downward from their penile sheath, which is between their hind legs. A female's urine stream jets backward from beneath her tail. When lactating females rear up on their hind legs, their nipples are readily apparent.

Size

In summer, an average-size mature female black bear in the Brooks Range of Alaska stands 24 to 30 inches tall at the shoulder, measures about 5 feet long from nose to tail, and weighs 120 to 140 pounds. Males average 200 to 300 pounds. In the same area, female grizzlies weigh 220 to 230 pounds, while males weigh 375 to 450 pounds.

In the Rockies, adult male grizzlies weigh 350 to 400 pounds in the spring; females average about 250 pounds. The bears gain 50 to 100 pounds by the time they den in the fall. An adult male will be 6 to 7 feet long and 30 to 36 inches high at the shoulder.

In midsummer, a mature, average-size male Kodiak bear is 7½ feet long, stands 4 feet high at the shoulder, and weighs 850 pounds. A female is 6½ feet long, stands 3½ feet tall at the shoulder, and weighs 450 pounds.

Speed

Black bears can run 25 to 30 miles per hour and grizzlies are even faster—35 miles per hour is a commonly used figure, and some published accounts say 41 miles per hour. By comparison, a fast high-school halfback runs a 40-yard dash in 4.5 seconds—that's 18.2 miles per hour. When you convert these figures into feet per second, the futility of trying to outrun a bear or climb a tree to safety to escape a charging bear is apparent. At 30 miles per hour, a bear covers 44 feet per second. If you're as fast as a high-school halfback, you're covering 26.67 feet per second. Let's say that after startling a bear that's 100 feet away, you panic and run. The bear gives chase. It's gaining 17 feet per second on you. In about 6 seconds, it will have you.

Senses
Vision

If you can see a bear, you should assume that it can see you.
—Steve French, Yellowstone Grizzly Foundation

The truism that bears have poor vision dates back at least to the days of the mountain men, but recently a number of bear researchers have given us an accurate and more complete picture on the visual acuity of bears. Grizzly and black bear vision has not been scientifically tested (Mr. Grizzly, would you please put a paw over your left eye and read the top line of the chart?), but the insights and observations of biologists provide valuable information that can help outdoors people avoid being seen by bears.[7]

In a chapter on grizzly bears for a second edition of the classic *Wild Mammals of North America*, Ph.D wildlife biologists Charles C. Schwartz, Sterling D. Miller, and Mark A. Haroldson write, "The popular myth that bears do not see well is contradicted by our personal observations

FACT OR FALLACY ?

FALLACY
Bears have poor vision.

FACT
There are reputable reports from biologists of bears seeing people more than a mile away. Bears key on movement and silhouette, and they notice bright colors.

of grizzly bears observing other bears or humans from distances of 1-2 km."[8]

Haroldson is a biologist with the Interagency Grizzly Bear Study Team (IGBST) in Bozeman, Montana. Schwartz did bear research for the Alaska Department of Fish and Game before taking the helm of the IGBST. Miller spent 23 years doing bear research for the Alaska Department of Fish & Game before joining the National Wildlife Federation staff in Missoula, Montana. He's a past president of the International Association for Bear Research and Management. Based on years of field experience, these biologists tell us bears are capable of spotting people more than a mile away.

In *Walking with Bears*, biologist Terry DeBruyn cautioned against comparing a bear's vision to its other senses: "Bears supposedly have poor eyesight, and, compared to their keen sense of smell and acute hearing, I agree the bear's vision is relatively poor. Nevertheless, although somewhat myopic, I believe bears have good vision. It is known that they see colors, which enables them to recognize and differentiate edible plants, fruits, and nuts."[9]

The belief that bears have poor vision is often based on misinterpretations of bear behavior. For example, the outdoors editor for an Alaskan newspaper tried to prove that bears have poor vision with the following anecdote: "Sitting still along a creek in Port Dick one year, I had a half dozen black bears walk by me within 25 feet without ever noticing." It's possible the bears didn't see him, but it's just as likely they saw him and ignored him.

The outdoors editor also claims that on several occasions, he stumbled upon sleeping bears while deer hunting on Kodiak Island. The bears looked up when they heard him. He froze. He "managed to back out of the area when the bears put their heads back down and returned to napping. That they would behave like this if they had seen a human seems surprising."[10]

Maybe not. In a 2005 article about bear vision published in the Alaska Department of Fish And Game's *Alaska Wildlife News,* biologist John Hechtel said, "A lot of times bears see things and don't visibly react by standing up or fleeing. That doesn't mean it didn't see it. People expect bears to react when they see something, and that's not always the case."

"Bears aren't wandering around half-blind," wrote Hechtel, adding that "seeing silhouette and movement is an important part of a bear's distance vision."[11]

In the same article, biologist Harry Reynolds described an incident that illustrates the bears' ability to spot movement and silhouettes at a considerable distance. Reynolds and another biologist spotted a large adult male grizzly that had killed and was eating a two-year-old grizzly. "It was late September and the ground was snow-covered when we peeked just our heads above a ridge that was a quarter-mile distant from the bears," Reynolds said. "The adult male immediately stopped what he was doing, stared in our direction, and ran." Reynolds notes that there was only a slight breeze, and it was not blowing from his back toward the bear. He's confident the bear didn't smell the men, it saw them. There's no telling whether the bear spotted the men's movement or noticed their silhouettes, but it did see them from a quarter-mile away. A 1937 report from Europe noted that brown bears in a zoo could see people at 120 yards and recognize their handler at 60 yards.[12]

Lyle Wilmarth, a research technician with the Colorado Division of Wildlife black bear studies, had a similar experience:

I was hunting mule deer near timberline on the upper end of an old logged area. I spotted a medium sized black bear crossing the logged area at a distance of 800 yards. I immediately sat down to observe the bear with binoculars. The bear apparently had seen me and he calmly walked to a small clump of trees, which he stopped behind. He held tight for several minutes as I watched. Finally he stuck his head through the limbs and looked directly at me. Within a few minutes he slowly moved off towards the ridgeline, always keeping good cover between himself and me.[13]

Larry Aumiller managed the Alaska Department of Fish and Game's McNeil River Sanctuary for Brown Bears for more than a quarter century. He got to watch and interact with bears in fairly open country. Aumiller told the *Alaska Wildlife News* he thinks "bears see on a par with humans up to about 120 yards, and beyond that their vision drops off."[14]

Of course, Aumiller is talking about the eyesight of average bears and average humans. There's considerable variation among individuals of both species. And visual acuity sometimes declines with age. Given that a hiker who spots a bear 180 yards away isn't likely to know whether the bear is young or old, or should be wearing glasses, it's best to assume the bear has average bear vision. It's safe to assume the bear can see you, especially if you're moving.

BYU professor Tom Smith emphasized the importance of movement and silhouette in an article about bear myths titled "The Bear That Never Was." Smith wrote that "[w]hile studying coastal black bears, Canadian researcher Tom Reimchen found that if he stood against a forest backdrop, bears passed through a nearby meadow without noticing him. If he slowly raised his arms, however, they immediately fixed their eyes on him."[15]

Wildlife biologist Stephen Stringham raised three orphaned black bear cubs in Alaska, which gave him a unique opportunity to observe their visual capabilities. In Stringham's book *Beauty Within the Beast,* he writes that the cubs "rarely noticed any bear approaching from downwind or behind us until he was within 50 yards... they were poor at spotting anything standing still or walking straight toward us—keeping its appearance nearly constant—while more than 50 yards away." [16]

This collection of observations about bear vision has practical implications for hikers and other outdoors people. Bears have color vision, and the brighter the clothes you're wearing, the better the odds a bear will notice you. It's clear that bears key on movement. A bear might not see a stationary person, but if you're moving, the bear is more likely to spot you. Side to side movement is more evident to bears than a direct approach or retreat. If you're standing still and there are trees, brush, or boulders right behind you that break up your silhouette, a bear might not notice you. If you're silhouetted on the skyline, you'll stick out like a sore thumb and a bear will probably spot you, particularly if you're moving.

You want to avoid being seen by nearby bears because when they become aware of your presence they might regard you as a threat and respond by charging. You want to avoid detection by distant bears because they might approach out of curiosity.

Hearing

Like bear vision, bear hearing has not been tested. Anecdotal evidence suggests that under optimal conditions bears can detect normal human conversation at distances of 300 yards or more.

Smell

Bears have a legendary sense of smell. In an article titled "Grizzlies Have Great Sniffers," Dr. George Stevenson, a retired neurosurgeon who's studying how a bear's brain works, said bears have "the greatest olfactory mechanism on earth...I think they smell their way through life."[17] Bears will stand up on their hind legs to smell and see better. Occasionally, they drop to all fours and circle downwind to confirm things.

Hibernation

No matter where you go in bear country, you need to understand the hibernation pattern in the region. Grizzly bears in the Brooks Range hibernate for six months of the year or more. A thousand miles to the south, on Kodiak Island, in some years a few bears do not hibernate at all. Some black bears in the South never hibernate, while black bears in Minnesota may spend seven months in their winter den. As you plan your visit, find out how late in the fall the bears might remain active and how early in the late winter/early spring they emerge from their dens.

Reproduction

Bears mate in the spring and early summer, and the female gives birth in the den during midwinter. Both black bear and brown bear cubs weigh less than a pound at birth. Litter size ranges from one to six and is typically two or three. Black bears generally stay with their mother for seventeen months. Grizzly cubs usually stay with their mother for 2 ½ years, or sometimes even 3 ½ years. Grizzlies have a low reproductive capacity because females don't breed until the age of 5 to 8 years, and then they care for their cubs for 2 to 3 years.

Food

Both black and grizzly bears are omnivores, but that doesn't mean they'll eat anything. Bears eat from a large variety of diverse food groups; however, they may only eat 10 to 25 percent of all the plant species available at a given location. Each plant is generally consumed at a particular time of year—for instance, black bears in Southeast Alaska eat rye grass along the beach in the spring, but feast on blueberries in the spruce forest during the fall. High calorie foods like salmon, acorns, and berries are far more important than low calorie foods.

BEHAVIOR

As more and more people crowd into bear country, the same intelligence and curiosity that helped black and grizzly bears survive through the ages often lead to conflicts with humans. Many problems result from our failure to store food securely or handle garbage properly, resulting in food-conditioned bears. This brings bears close to people, and people are generally intolerant of bears.

Personal Space, Territory, and Home Range

"Grizzlies will attack to defend cubs, their territory, or a carcass they're feeding on."

—Caroline Frasier, *Outside* magazine[18]

Personal space, territory, and *home range* are not interchangeable terms. Personal space is the area that, if entered, will cause and animal to fight or flee. Most grizzly-bear-related human injuries are a direct con-

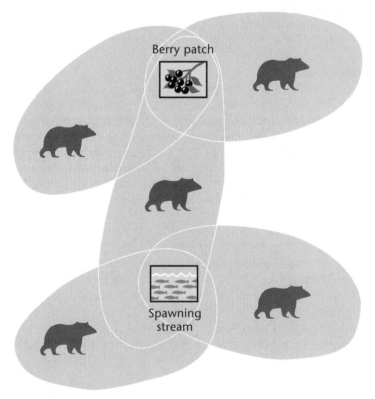

A grizzly lives in a home range that overlaps the home ranges of other bears. Grizzlies don't defend their home ranges from other grizzlies–or people.

sequence of a person encroaching on a grizzly bears' personal space. Territorial animals defend a specific area from their own species. Wolf pack A won't allow Wolf pack B into its territory. They scent-mark an exclusive territory; howling sometimes functions as a verbal picket fence—keep out of our territory. During nesting season, bald eagles guard an exclusive territory around their nest. In *Bears Of Alaska in Life and Legend*, Alaska Department of Fish & Game biologist Harry V. Reynolds, a past president of the IBA, wrote, "Grizzlies do not occupy and defend fixed territories but they do live in fairly well-defined areas call 'home ranges.' The home range of one bear may overlap broadly with those of other grizzlies."[19]

Home ranges vary in size from about 40 square miles on Alaska's food-rich Admiralty Island, to over 600 square miles in places like the *Arctic National Wildlife Refuge,* where food is not only less abundant, but widely dispersed on a seasonal basis. Throughout most of their range, black bears are not territorial; however, there are areas, mostly east of the Mississippi River, where black bears do defend an exclusive territory—from other black bears, not people. Food is quite abundant in these locations, and a bear can live on just a few square miles of land.

Intelligence

Doug Suess, who trains bears for movies and television shows, points out that you only have to show bears how to do something one time, maybe twice, and they've got it.[20] In Yosemite, that kind of intelligence has given us bears that specialize at breaking into a particular make, model, and year of car. Once a bear figures out how to rip open the door on a 1997 Toyota Corolla, you're out of luck if you park yours at a trailhead. In the backcountry, if a bear happens to find food in a pack at your campsite, it's likely to return again and again to look for food in the packs of other campers. One mistake and you train the bear to bother other campers.

Curious bears often make a slow, halting approach toward people, other bears, and intriguing objects. They crane their neck, their ears are cocked forward, their head and nose are up, and they sniff, sniff, sniff.

In Denali, where food-conditioned bears are a rarity, most property damage stems from bears just checking things out—your tent, for example. While you're gone on a day hike, a grizzly will come along and give a tentative push on your tent with its paw. It's easy to imagine the bear's thoughts at this point: "Wow. It springs right back. This is fun. I wonder what would happen if I bit this thing?" It doesn't take much effort for a grizzly to bite a free-standing tent, pick it up, shake it, and

Yellowstone Park's caption for this photo says, "Tent that was jumped on by a grizzly bear (nicknamed Kelty) in Indian Creek Campground."

just have a good old time. Bears in Denali destroy several tents every summer in this manner. They're just curious.

One of bear expert Doug Peacock's favorite stories involves a bear that made its way into a Park Service patrol cabin in Glacier National Park. It bit into cans of ham and baked beans and almost all the other goodies it found—but not the cans of sauerkraut.

Biologist Tom Beck notes that "a wide variety of petroleum-based smells, like lantern and propane stove fuel, attract bears. In fact, the additive put in natural gas to make it a noticeable odor has been used to successfully lure in bears during bear baiting operations."[21]

Several biologists report that bears have bitten campers' fuel bottles; if you take a stove and fuel bottle on your outdoor excursions, play it safe and store them with your food and garbage.

I wouldn't go so far as to say bears have a rubber fetish, but they do have a thing about rubber rafts, polyethylene kayaks, foam sleeping pads, and buoys from crab pots. If an object has any spring or bounce, a bear is likely to play with it. This includes plastic and Styrofoam ice chests because they give a little before they break. It doesn't matter whether you have a brand new ice chest or one that reeks of fish; they're all fun for bears. Plastic water bottles are fair game, too.

Anyone who's done much kayaking along the coast of Southeast Alaska or British Columbia knows that you can do everything right— cook below the high-tide line, store your food and odorous items in a bear can, and pitch your tent 100 yards upwind from your food storage area—and when you wake up in the morning, tracks in the mud and sand will tell you that a bear walking along the beach at night noticed your tent, made a detour for it, checked things out, and then went back the way it came.

One year the biologists at Alaska's McNeil River cut and stacked a few driftwood logs on a beach in front of their quarters. Bears had been walking by the uncut and scattered logs all summer, but now they had something new in their environment. They scattered the firewood. They couldn't stay away from it. There's nothing malicious about the curiosity of bears. It evolved as a food-finding strategy. It's perfectly natural behavior. Bears are so curious they'll try almost anything once—except sauerkraut.

Bears are curious and will investigate almost anything new in their world. They often sniff, paw, and then bite new objects.

FACT OR FALLACY ?

FALLACY
Bears are unpredictable.

FACT
For the most part bears are predictable, but few people know enough about bear behavior in general, let alone the quirks of individual bears, to predict what any bear will do in a given situation. "Black bears are not unpredictable," says biologist Terry Debruyn. "They are predictable. What complicates our predictions is that bears are individuals with individual personalities."[22]

Predictability

In *Living with Bears,* Stephen Herrero says, "If you've studied an individual bear, its behavior is almost 100 percent predictable. The bear has developed certain set ways to respond to danger, challenge, opportunity, (and) obstacles."[23] Labeling bears as unpredictable just shuts the door to knowledge and understanding.

In *River of Bears,* photographer Johnny Johnson gives an account of longtime McNeil River manager Larry Aumiller using his knowledge of an individual brown bear to predict what it would do. Aumiller and a group of people encountered a bear named Regina. "While she was still quite some distance away, Larry said, 'She'll give us a little rush when she gets closer.' Sure enough, ten minutes later she put on this little charge, and Larry stepped forward and yelled, 'No!' Regina stopped still, and then went on her way completely ignoring us thereafter. Larry looked at me, laughed, and said, 'They're so predictable.'"[24]

So many people have said that bears are unpredictable that novice outdoors people now believe they're at the whim of chance in bear country. Why store food properly? Why worry about the odors of cooking food? No matter what you do, a bear could put you in the hospital. It's just fate. When you believe bears are unpredictable, it's easy to get a dangerous "what difference does it make?" attitude. Your actions count. It's easy to predict you'll cause trouble if you step inside a bear's personal space or let it get your food.

Some (but not all) bears quickly habituate to humans. They learn to ignore a recurring stimulus such as hikers on a trail if there's no reward involved. When bears are rewarded with food, they become food-conditioned. Sometimes food-conditioned bears approach people or campsites in the same manner as curious bears, but they can also be quite bold. They know what they want—your food—and they can be pushy. Black bears will actually make threat displays toward people who block their way to food.

Bear Interaction and Communication

When you look at photos or film footage of a congregation of bears fishing for salmon at a place like McNeil River or Brooks River in Katmai National Park, you'll often see two bears fighting or standing just inches apart jawing at each other in a tense situation. When you visit those places yourself, what you see is that smaller bears usually get out of the way of bigger bears and that's that. Even between bears of equal size, serious fights are the exception to the rule. It's almost as though each bear is charged like the positive end of a magnet; whenever two bears get close to each other, they don't touch because the magnetic field keeps them a safe distance apart.

When bears do get close enough for a confrontation, they exhibit signs of stress and use vocalizations and body language to communicate with each other. This prevents fights that could cause serious injuries or death. Yawning indicates low-level stress. Grizzlies tend to slobber—a bit of foam on the lips—when they're stressed, but this is uncommon with black bears.

If you quickly inhale and instantly blow out so hard your cheeks puff out, you'll imitate the "blowing" sound that black bears commonly make. With grizzly bears it comes out as a "woof." Blowing or woofing may be accompanied by clacking teeth. One bear might blow and make a short lunge toward another bear while slapping its paws on the ground or a tree. Although bears roar during fights, they rarely growl, and they never growl to threaten others. There are reports of bears growling at people during close encounters, but in the "Language and Sounds of Black Bears," biologist Lynn Rogers notes that "[f]earful people often describe any bear sound as a growl."[25]

When a young male grizzly gets too close to a mature female with cubs, she might regard him as a threat to her offspring and charge him. He's going to meet her charge with his head down, mouth open, ears back, and his hindquarters lowered in a slight crouch. He signals that he's unwilling to attack, yet ready to defend himself. She probably won't make contact because she doesn't want to start what could be a fatal fight.

After introductions, they stand there and make open mouth threats at each other. He can't make any sudden moves or attempt to back away. He can't break off the encounter because she's the dominant bear and

Opposite: When grizzly bears are stressed, they tend to froth at the mouth and salivate.

he's the subordinate. If he shows any signs of submission, she might pounce on him. He has to meet her first threat with a threat of his own, and even after the initial tension dissipates he's in a delicate position. He can't retreat, he doesn't want to threaten her so much he provokes an attack, yet he must somehow convey that he's ready and willing to defend himself. He does that just by standing there, by not retreating. Standing still signals an unwillingness to attack. He'll probably lower his head very slowly and look at the ground while watching her out of the corner of his eye. She knows he won't attack her, so she can look and move around. Eventually, she'll leave.

Although female bears with cubs will charge large, dominant males, the bear that approaches another bear is usually in control of the situation. During an encounter, bears huff, pant, sniff, walk with their front legs stiffened, lay their ears back, pop their jaws, circle each other, vocalize, and exhibit all sorts of other behaviors. When Alaska Department of Fish and Game biologist Derek Stonorov studied brown bear behavior at McNeil River in the early 1970s for his master's thesis, he found that they routinely used at least forty visual signals to communicate.[26]

There are three key behaviors you need to be aware of:
1. The bear that approaches is usually in command of the situation.
2. The subordinate bear does not end an engagement with a dominant bear; the dominant bear is the first to leave.
3. Merely standing still has signal value: standing still will often alter the ongoing behavior of an approaching bear.

Based on the dynamics of bear–bear encounters, I stand my ground when approached by a bear during a sudden, close-up encounter. I also stand my ground when approached by curious or food-conditioned bears. I'll even clap my hands or act more aggressively toward curious or food-conditioned bears if they persist in coming closer. Such techniques, however, warrant more detail and are discussed in a later chapter, "Close Encounters."

There is no research or scientific evidence to indicate that human sexual practices might attract bears.

Menstruation, Sex, and Bears

It is well known that odors attract bears. But is there any proof that the odors of menstruation or sex are more attractive to bears than the odors of smelly socks or the sweat-soaked shoulder straps of your pack?

MENSTRUATION

"Although evidence is inconclusive, menstrual odors and human sexual activity may attract bears."

—Glacier National Park, 2006

"There is no scientific evidence to suggest that menstrual odors precipitate grizzly bear attacks."

—Steve French, Yellowstone Grizzly Foundation

Ever since Glacier National Park's infamous "night of the grizzlies" in 1967, menacing warnings that imply menstrual odors attract bears have needlessly worried women or kept them out of bear country altogether. These warnings have created a fear far out of proportion to the risk. In 1992, however, the Interagency Grizzly Bear Committee (IGBC) began distributing a brochure titled "Women in Bear Country" that states, "There is no evidence that grizzlies are overly attracted to menstrual odors more than they are any other odor and there is no statistical evidence that known attacks have been related to menstruation."

I'm pleased the IGBC is finally trying to set the record straight, but it's probably too late. The menstrual myth is too well established. While there are usually a multitude of possible explanations for a bear attack and many contributing factors, I suspect that ten, twenty, even fifty years from now, if a bear attacks a woman, some people will say, "I'll bet she was menstruating."

Because government brochures have often relied on innuendo and insinuation to convey information about bears and menstruation, discussions of this delicate topic tend to be long on rumors and short on facts. Let's go back to the "night of the grizzlies" and get all the facts so that women can make an informed decision on whether or not to travel in bear country while menstruating.

Night of the Grizzlies

On August 13, 1967, two women were killed by grizzly bears in separate incidents in two different backcountry areas of Glacier National Park. Because these were Glacier Park's first bear-related deaths, they attracted intense media coverage and immense public interest. It was a strange and disturbing coincidence that both deaths occurred on the same night and involved young women. "The mystery," reported an article in *Sports Illustrated*, "triggered almost hysterical speculation as to the cause."[1]

Investigators found two common environmental factors: garbage and menstruation. Both bears were addicted to garbage; in the vernacular of biologists, they were food-conditioned bears. The bruins had a long history of visiting backcountry camping areas where they obtained food scraps, discarded food containers, and even the remains of fish caught by campers. The second common environmental factor was menstruation. One women was carrying tampons, which led investigators to the conclusion that her period was about to begin. The other woman was actually menstruating.

Although it was well known that garbage attracted grizzlies and often brought them in close proximity with humans, no scientific field research had ever been conducted to determine whether menstrual odors attracted bears or might somehow cause a bear attack. Still, folklore had it that stallions are upset by menstruating women, and menstrual blood had been blamed for triggering shark attacks on women. It wasn't long before the investigators received a number of letters from various people around the country reporting incidents of menstruating women being attacked by a variety of animals.

This reminds me of a 1995 Associated Press news release titled "Smelly Socks Attract Grizzly." After a day of hiking, a hunter in British Columbia took his shoes and socks off to cool his feet. "The bear, he figures, picked up his scent from the smelly socks. 'Within two minutes of me putting my shoes and socks back on and heading back up the trail, the sow came at me full blast from the side,' he said."[2]

This incident doesn't prove smelly socks attract bears any more than a few letters from the public prove animals attack menstruating women. Perhaps the letters sent to Glacier Park provided interesting or amusing reading for biologists and agency officials trying to determine the cause of Glacier's bear attacks; however, they had better evidence to consider:

> On the night of August 13, 1967, two young women [both menstruating], three young men, and one dog were camped together at Trout Lake. The bear approached the camp several times, first at 8:00 p.m. as it was getting dark and after the campers had cooked hot dogs and fish. The bear frightened the campers so they abandoned their campsite and moved their sleeping bags down to the lake. The bear seemed most interested in their food, as had been the case with previous visitors to Trout Lake.
>
> On the bear's final visit, when all the campers were asleep in their sleeping bags, it approached and examined each in turn. Michele Koons was the last person the bear approached. The other four got out of their bags and were jumping and shouting, causing confusion and excitement as they rushed to climb trees. In this atmosphere of noise and excitement, the bear went directly to the one remaining person and almost immediately began tearing into her sleeping bag. Michele couldn't get her zipper undone and could not get out of her bag (USDI 1967).[3]

What initially attracted the bear to the camping area? I'd say it was the bear's previous experience with food and garbage—not menstrual odors. Having the bear so close to the campers set the stage for disaster, but what attracted the bear to Michele Koons? If menstrual odors attract bears, why was the victim the last person the bear visited? Why didn't the bear just ignore the men and go directly for the menstruating women? Why did the bear ignore menstruating woman No. 1 and single out Michele Koons?

Just for the sake of argument, let's say the bear's previous success at obtaining food from hikers at Trout Lake is what initially brought it into the campsite, and the odor of menstruation is the factor that ultimately attracted the bear to Michele Koons. Our next question, then, is, What enticed the bear to attack? Was it menstrual odors? Food odors that saturated her clothes while cooking hot dogs and fish? Michele Koons was also a heavy user of cosmetics. Did the odor of cosmetics cause the attack? What about the shouting and confusion? Did Michele Koons make a sudden movement or a loud noise that caught the bear's attention? How can you pick one factor, isolate it from all other factors, and say, "This is what triggered the attack"?

You can't. Yet the final report on Michele Koons' death mentioned that "[a] number of letters have been received at the Park reporting incidents of women in their monthly period being attacked by various wild animals. It would seem a plausible reason for the attack."[4]

The Agencies React

It must have seemed very plausible indeed, because the Park Service and other agencies began to include menstrual warnings in bear brochures and pamphlets distributed to the public. Several Canadian parks also began publishing menstrual warnings.

I'm sure the Park Service and other agencies were genuinely concerned that menstruating women might be at greater risk than other people in bear country. Still, given the complete absence of scientific research on menstrual odors and bears at the time, it seems difficult to justify a decision to publish written menstrual warnings. I'm convinced the primary reason menstrual warnings found their way into print is that government agencies were concerned about protecting themselves from liability for bear attacks. There have been at least seven attempts to sue the U.S. government for negligence in incidents involving bear attacks. In my opinion, the intent of the menstrual warnings was to foil potential lawsuits. In the rare event that a bear attacked a menstruating woman, government lawyers could always tell a judge, "We warned her."

Biologists eventually convinced agencies to remove menstrual warnings from brochures, but then a 1980 study on polar bears by University of Montana graduate student Bruce Cushing brought the issue to the forefront again. I'm going to discuss the study in detail because it provides the only scientific evidence we have that menstrual odors attract bears.[5]

One part of the study tested the responses of polar bears to both menstruating and nonmenstruating women. The bears were kept at a laboratory in Churchill, Manitoba. One at a time, the polar bears were put in a 20-by-20-foot cage in a room equipped with an observation booth.

Just outside the bars of the cage, food and odorous items were randomly placed in one of two "fan boxes." Seal oil, human blood, chicken, used tampons, seafood, and other items were placed in the boxes and the fans were run for 20 minutes. Although bears could scent the food, they couldn't reach it. During a 20-minute test period, each bear's behavior was recorded for 10 seconds at the start of every minute.

A "maximum response" was defined as "sniffs for most of the test, tracks scent to source, and shows from 5 to 10 minutes of increased activity" such as pacing the cage, pawing, chewing on the bars, chuffing, and sniffing. When a bear sniffed several times and showed increased activity for 2 minutes or less, this was considered a "moderate response." A "minimum response" occurred if the bear sniffed the air three to seven times but didn't move. If there was no movement but the bear sniffed the air ten to twenty times, its response was listed as "minimum-plus."

In tests with women instead of food, the women sat passively by the fan boxes for 20 minutes. The bear in the cage could see the women. With nonmenstruating women, there was one moderate, one minimum-plus, and three minimum responses. With menstruating women, there were six moderate and one minimum response.

Bears did not respond to human blood or unused tampons. Bears did respond to used tampons. There were four maximum responses and one minimum-plus response. One bear slept through the test.

Cushing also observed the reaction of wild bears in an outdoor setting to various food and scents. Plain paper toweling was used to hold 5 milliliters or less of seafood, chicken, blood, and other attractants fixed to forty-two stakes that were widely dispersed in the vicinity of an observation tower. In addition, both used and unused tampons were attached to some of these stakes. The amount of menstrual blood was not measured or controlled. Observers watched forty-five bears approach the stakes 150 times.

When bears approached within 30 yards of the stakes from a downwind direction, they scented seafood 100 percent of the time, chicken 80 percent, seal oil 73 percent, used tampons 65 percent, and human blood 17 percent. After scenting the attractants, the bears usually investigated the bait stations. The consumption rate was 100 percent for chicken, 92 percent for seal oil, 66 percent for beer, 62 percent for seafood, 54 percent for used tampons, and 13 percent for unused tampons.

Based on the results of these tests, Cushing reached the following conclusions:

[M]enstrual odors attract bears.... It is some aspect peculiar to menstrual blood which elicits this attraction.

Although menstrual odors attract polar bears, we must avoid drawing the simple conclusion that attacks upon menstruating women will occur. The odor test did not take into account the physical presence of human beings [and] the bears, in general, appeared to attempt to avoid or escape the women. This was true in 11 of 12 trials.

Polar bears in the wild would be attracted by menstrual odors, but it is impossible to predict their further actions. Because of other behavioral traits, they may retreat upon discovering the individual, as the test animals in the laboratory usually did. I recommend the following:

- For the present, assume that all bears are attracted to menstrual odors, but plan now for investigating this relationship with regard to the other species of bears as soon as possible.
- Agencies and companies should issue firm warnings and take positive steps to protect human females required to work in bear habitat or who utilize bear habitat for other reasons.

Shortly after the results of Cushing's research were made public, a headline in the October 26, 1980, *Great Falls Tribune* read "Bear Attacks, Menstruation Link Proven."

Copies of the study were distributed for review with Glacier National Park employees. A November 13, 1980, memo from the park's wilderness specialist to the administrative officer said that "it seems timely that we address some potential problems we may now foresee in assigning women employees to backcountry locations."[6]

As you can probably predict, this memo prompted quite a few other memos, and meetings, and high anxiety at high levels of the NPS bureaucracy. There were Equal Employment Opportunity committee meetings and personnel meetings. Lawyers reviewed the facts. Even the director of the NPS wrote memos about women, menstruation, and bears.

Cushing's research was carefully scrutinized. Most people saw one problem right away: Polar bears are 99 percent carnivorous, whereas black and grizzly bears are omnivorous; they consume far more plants than do polar bears. Another issue was that Cushing's results were based, in part, on how four different polar bears responded to a total of twelve encounters with menstruating and nonmenstruating women—that's a tiny sample size. A group of nine women who worked in Glacier Park pointed out a few other problems:[7]

1. In lab tests, the form of the women was visible to the bear. It's not clear whether the bear was responding to the form of a human or an odor.
2. Cushing suggested that one possible explanation for the bears' interest in used tampons and menstrual odors might be that bears recognize and investigate sexual odors. He emphasized that research would be needed to verify this hypothesis. It can't be assumed that only women have hormonal cycles. Evidence indicates that men have hormonal cycles, too, and any research would need to explore both possibilities.
3. "The methodology employed by Cushing . . . was not scientifically sound." Cushing observed the responses of bears to used tampons. The fluid held within a tampon has a strong odor when it makes contact with bacteria in the air and starts to decompose. Only menstrual blood was tested in the tampons. The results might have been the same with any type of human blood placed in tampons, or human blood in oysters for that matter.

The NPS had doubts about the validity of Cushing's research and apprehension about the legal ramifications of his recommendations. A November 17, 1980, memo from the acting superintendent of Glacier Park to the NPS associate regional director concerning Backcountry Assignments for Female Employees said, "We are hesitant to develop any policy statements on our own.... [I]t may be best addressed at least Regionally and possibly at the Washington level. It may also warrant a Solicitor's opinion. Our reaction is that the bear informational handout material should be revised [to] include these findings and be included in all seasonal employee packets. This may serve to ease the liability implications. However, due to EEO and Privacy Act implications, the determination of whether to bring up the subject or not with a supervisor should be left up to the female employee."

The NPS was in a quandary. Because of "liability implications," NPS officials felt they had to warn park visitors that it might be dangerous for menstruating women to travel in bear country. At the same time, the NPS had to tell employees that it was safe for menstruating women to work in bear country. It was clear there would be lawsuits for sexual discrimination if the NPS refused to hire women for jobs in bear country.

A 1981 memo from the director of the NPS to the Rocky Mountain Regional Director said that "based upon.... the fact that research has not clearly demonstrated that there is a correlation between menstrual odor and bear attraction, we do not believe policy should be established to control assignment of female employees to backcountry areas. In view of the lack of conclusive research.... we would be subject of complaints of differential treatment."[8]

In a management directive concerning women in the backcountry, the superintendent of Glacier National Park wrote that the results of Bruce Cushing's polar bear studies "were inconclusive and the applicability of the thesis to Glacier's grizzly and black bears is questionable, and will remain so until further research is conducted."[9]

Although Glacier Park officials told employees that the results of Cushing's research were "inconclusive," their bear literature warned the public that "odors attract bears.... menstruating women may choose to stay out of bear country." As a matter of practical policy, Glacier Park officials were warning female visitors to stay out of bear country during their menstrual periods, yet hiring women to work as backcountry rangers. There were black bears and menstruating women in national forests all over the country, yet only a few Montana forests distributed written menstrual warnings. Women in Yellowstone Park received menstrual warnings; women in Yosemite did not. Glacier, yes. Great Smoky Mountains, no.

Double standards, hypocrisy, and inconsistent policies fostered skepticism about menstrual warnings. As the years went by, a variety of studies investigated the theory that menstrual odors attract bears. In *Bear Attacks: Their Cause and Avoidance,* Dr. Stephen Herrero said, "[I]n my analysis of grizzly-bear-inflicted injury, I did not find a correlation between attacks on women and any particular stage of their menstrual cycles."[10]

In 1991, longtime black bear biologist Dr. Lynn L. Rogers published a research paper titled "Reactions of Black Bears to Human Menstrual Odors." He did fieldwork, asked the question of hundreds of fellow biologists gathered for a bear conference, and reviewed existing bear literature. His conclusions: "Menstrual odors were essentially ignored by black bears.... In an extensive review of black bear attacks across North America, we found no instance of black bears attacking or being attracted to menstruating women."[11]

In 1994, Yellowstone Park's bear management office released an information paper that examined the statistics on bear-related injuries from 1980 to 1994. Of more than 600,000 visitor-use nights in the backcountry, "Twenty-one people were injured by bears within the park.... [O]f these 21 injuries, 15 (71%) were men, and 6 (29%) were women. Most (86%) of these injuries involved sudden, close encounters between bear and hiker and were therefore probably unrelated to menstruation. Of the three (14%) incidents where people were injured while camping, two of the injured people were male and one was female. The woman was not menstruating at the time of the attack. There was no evidence linking menstruation to any of these 21 bear attacks."[12]

THE NOSE KNOWS

In *River of Bears,* biologist Larry Aumiller describes a bear interaction that shows how much bears trust their noses—and convinced me that a bear is capable of detecting a woman's menstrual odors. During mating season, male bears track females in estrus by scent. Aumiller watched as a female, being scent-tracked by a male, doubled back around the edge of a gravel spit and passed quite close to the boar. The male was on one side of a spit, the female was on the other. He spotted her, paused, and looked at her. Instead of taking a shortcut directly across the spit toward her, the male put his nose back to the ground and went way out of his way as he continued to follow her by scent.[13]

There's no question in my mind that a bear's nose can distinguish menstrual odors from other odors. But there's no evidence bears are attracted to menstrual odors more than any other odor. Even if bears were attracted to menstrual odors, that attractiveness is clearly outweighed by a bear's customary avoidance of humans. A bear that smells menstrual odors from a woman camped in a tent doesn't move in to investigate because the bear also smells the woman, her companions, and other things human.

A Commonsense Approach

With all the research that's been done, I believe Caroline Byrd's 1988 master's thesis gives us by far the most thorough analysis of Cushing's research and the whole topic of menstrual odors attracting bears. She warns us that "making the jump from menstruation attracting bears to menstruation causing bear attacks is inappropriate" because so many factors influence the outcome of any encounter between bears and humans.[14]

After reviewing Cushing's field tests with used tampons, seal oil, and other attractants, Byrd says "this still does not answer the question of whether or not bears are attracted to menstruating women. A menstruating woman does not smell like a used tampon. Menstrual flow has an odor only if it has been exposed to the air for some time. Cushing's results suggest [the] need for proper care and disposal of used tampons when in bear country, but they do not clearly indicate that polar bears are attracted to menstruating women."

Byrd also presents a powerful and thoughtful argument that our cultural attitudes toward menstruation predispose people to accept the premise that menstrual odors attract bears. Finally, Byrd conducted a statistical analysis of hundreds of documented bear encounters and the handful of fatal attacks to determine whether bears behaved differently around women and men. Her conclusion? "The question of whether menstruating women attract bears has not been answered.... Statistical analyses of bear/human encounters seem to indicate that bears do not respond significantly differently to men or women. Case-by-case analyses do not reveal menstruation playing a role in human female's encounters with bears, but there is much missing and unknowable information. Given the nature of the question, it cannot be said with confidence that bears are, or are not, attracted to menstrual odors."

In other words, statistics tell us that menstrual odors don't attract bears, or that the attractiveness of menstrual (and other) odors is usually offset by a bear's reluctance to get too close to people. Furthermore, given the nature of grizzly bears, it's extremely difficult to do field tests that prove menstrual odors don't attract grizzlies. We'll never be 100 percent sure about these things. Based on all the evidence we have about menstruation and bears, I offer the following thoughts and advice.

1. Use tampons, not sanitary pads if at all possible. If you do opt to use pads, be aware that this will cause additional odor a bear might notice. Every odor counts in bear country.
2. Use unscented tampons or pads rather than the deodorant type.
3. Use OB brand or similar tampons to eliminate odorous waste from plastic and cardboard applicators.
4. Wash your hands after changing and handling tampons or pads.
5. Store used tampons or pads as carefully as you store food, garbage, and other odorous items. Use bear cans or hang them with your garbage at least 4 feet from a tree trunk and 10 feet off the ground. As an extra precaution, keep used tampons or pads in airtight resealable plastic bags.
6. Treat soiled garments (underwear, etc.) as you would food and garbage.
7. Do not bury pads or tampons in the backcountry. Bears have keen noses. They might smell buried pads or tampons and dig them up.

8. Bear literature often advises women to burn used tampons in a hot fire, but a biologist with the Alaska Department of Fish and Game tried that and found that it's impossible. There's no way you can completely burn a used tampon. If you do burn used tampons to reduce (not eliminate) odors, remove charred remains of them from the fire pit and store them with other garbage.

Once Cushing's polar bear research was released, it's easy to understand why the agencies felt compelled to put some sort of menstrual information in bear brochures; they just did a lousy job of it. They overreacted. The IGBC's "Women in Bear Country" brochure states that "bears can sense fear." For almost thirty years, millions of visitors to national parks and forests have been handed literature with warnings that cause women to fear bears. Fortunately, that situation is changing. IGBC headquarters is trying to persuade all IGBC members to update their bear brochures. Yellowstone already has published an excellent information paper, "Bears and Menstruating Women." Women who might have been put off by scary menstrual warnings in the past can now get accurate facts and enjoy bear country.

SEX IN THE WILD

When I was at the McNeil River State Game Sanctuary watching bears with a small group of people led by Alaska Department of Fish and Game biologist Derek Stonorov, I mentioned that some bear literature claims human sexual behavior may attract bears.

Derek lives in Homer, Alaska, a small town featured in Tom Bodett's *The End of the Road*. It's an hour's flight from the end of the road to McNeil, where Derek escorts ten people a day to McNeil River Falls, home of the greatest concentration of brown bears on earth. As many as sixty-eight bears at a time have been seen feeding on chum salmon at the falls. Derek has been at McNeil on and off since the early 1970s, when he wrote his master's thesis on bear behavior. Derek knows bears. He keeps up on scientific bear literature. But because Derek lives at the end of the road, I wasn't surprised he hadn't heard about sex warnings in the Lower 48 states. When I mentioned the sex warnings, Derek gave me a quizzical look and asked, "Are you serious?"

"Yep," I said, "but I've never found any studies on the topic. I've asked the agencies that give sex warnings for references. I've asked more than once. No response. What a great research project for an intrepid grad student."

To the amusement of our entire group, Derek began thinking out loud.

"Can you imagine the exit survey for backpackers leaving bear country? 'Excuse me, did you engage in sex? Are either of you especially vocal? Do you tend to, uh, thrash around quite a bit? Did you use condoms?'"

If you think about it, we're often told to make noise to avoid surprising bears; during sex, people make all kinds of noise. You're supposed to shout at a black bear entering your camp; during sex, some people shout and yell. If you're in a close-up encounter with a grizzly, you should talk quietly to the bear; after sex, people often talk quietly with each other. Maybe human sexual activity deters bears. Maybe it attracts them. Maybe smelly socks attract bears. Nobody knows. And because nobody knows, agencies have no justification for publishing written warnings that say "human sexual practices may attract bears."

The sex myth originated in Glacier National Park in 1980, when rangers found the remains of a young man and woman killed by a bear. They were naked. In the first edition of *Bear Attacks: Their Causes and Avoidance*, biologist Stephen Herrero wrote, "The bear might have approached the teenagers because of the odors from sexual intercourse, but whether this was the cause and what happened next are conjecture."

I can't help wondering if "just say no" to sex in the wild is another way of saying you don't want your tent to smell like Cupid's gym. Now that's a legitimate concern. Fluids are also a legitimate concern. If you're so unimaginative or inexperienced you can't think of any human sexual practices that will keep odors to a minimum and eliminate liquids, don't have sex in bear country until you call Dr. Ruth.

chapter
4

Cooking and Food Storage

To him almost everything is food except granite.
—John Muir, *"Bears,"* 1901

FACT
Bears do have remarkably diverse diets, but they only eat about one out of every ten plants. More importantly, high-calorie seasonal foods are what count. Hikers in grizzly country are wise to avoid stands of whitebark pine in the fall because grizzlies from miles around gather to feast on the seeds from whitebark pine cones. When a spring freeze ruins a berry crop that would normally ripen in autumn, resource managers can predict bear-human conflicts will escalate in fall. No natural food will substitute for those berries, so bears invade the suburbs looking for other high-calorie food.

John Muir was wrong. When it comes to natural foods, bears are rather finicky. Out of 1,000 types of plants in a given area, they might only consume 100 to 250, and each of those will be eaten during a particular season. Yet as my friend Mark Jefferson discovered on a kayaking trip in southeast Alaska, bears will try to taste almost anything once.

Jefferson is a lunatic of sorts, a beady-eyed accountant–turned–computer programmer who's fond of slightly crazed outdoor adventures. During a recent Alaskan kayak trip, Jefferson left his campsite for "a minute" and, when he returned a half-hour later, the black bear that had destroyed his tent was now casually picking through the debris. Jefferson chased the bear off and surveyed the damage. There were gaping holes in his tent, insulation from his sleeping bag adorned the beach grass and nearby alders, and all of his food had been eaten, but what really annoyed Jefferson is that the bear had bitten his portable Macintosh computer. "I could see indents and scratches from his teeth," Mark told me.

I didn't ask Mark why he took a computer with him on a kayaking trip in Alaska—as I mentioned earlier, he's a lunatic—but this "modern-day Mac attack" illustrates that bears will taste-test almost anything.

HOW BEARS BECOME FOOD-CONDITIONED

Because bears are curious, intelligent, powerful, and endlessly searching for food, improper food storage is the root cause of many conflicts and confrontations between bears and humans. State and federal land agencies publish brochures with slogans like "a fed bear is a dead bear" or "garbage kills bears," and these slogans often prove true. Hikers and active outdoors people often think it's other people—the suburban family "camping" in a 38-foot-long air-conditioned RV—who corrupt bears with hot dogs and chips, but a 1980 study in Yosemite National Park found that while 92 percent of all backpackers said they stored their food correctly, only 3 percent actually did.[2]

The chain of events that turns fed bears into dead bears is depressingly familiar to bear aficionados. A family from Anywhere USA rents an RV and drives to Banff National Park in Alberta, Canada. They leave a bag of groceries on the picnic table when they go to an evening ranger talk. When they return, scraps of paper and plastic are strewn everywhere, but all the fixings for turkey sandwiches are gone, consumed by a black bear that now associates this campground area with food. A day later, the bear returns, only this time there are people watching. The bear is nervous. It would probably run if someone shouted or took a quick step toward it. Instead, someone tosses the bear a bag of potato chips. Now the bear associates both the campground and people with food. The next time it returns, banging together pots and pans probably won't deter the bear. Even if you blew off firecrackers, the bear might not leave, at least not for long. It's been rewarded with food and it's coming back for more. At this particular campground, a certain tolerance for humans replaces the bear's initial caution around people. It could be more likely to risk getting close to people at other locations, too.

This bear doesn't have long to live. Maybe it will wander into a hunter's camp outside the park and get shot. It might start approaching backpackers and be "removed from the population" by a land management agency. Someone at the campground might try to grab food back from the bear and get cuffed in retaliation. If a person is seriously injured, or sometimes just scared, we retaliate by killing the bear. Fed bears are often dead bears.

The big picture here is that bears weigh positive gains (food) versus the risk of injury, hassles with people, and other negative factors. When the positive outweighs the negative, the bear will seek food. When the negative outweighs the positive, the bear will move on. Storing food properly is the single most important thing you can do to prevent conflicts between bears and humans.

FACT OR FALLACY ?

FALLACY
Bears are nocturnal.

FACT
In *A Shadow in the Forest: Idaho's Black Bear,* biologists John Beecham and Jeff Rohlman wrote, "Black bears were originally thought to be nocturnal animals because they were often seen at night around campgrounds and summer homes. However, our telemetry studies clearly showed that these activity patterns were an adaptation to the presence of humans and that wild bears in natural settings are seldom active at night."

In other words, nocturnal activity is often just a bear's way of avoiding the hubbub of human activity during the day. The less human disturbance in an area, the more active bears will be during the day, especially at dawn and dusk. There's nothing "wrong" with a bear that's out and about during the day. Bears will switch to nocturnal feeding to avoid the heat of the day, especially in hot country like the Southwestern United States.

I've heard people whine about how much trouble it is to store food in bear country, but if you don't use the same basic techniques when camping on the Havasupai Reservation in the Grand Canyon, ringtail cats will get your food. Raccoons and skunks will raid your food cache in places like Kentucky and Tennessee. Regardless of where you camp, some precautions will probably be necessary to protect your food from hungry critters.

Stern warnings about bears, food, and garbage have given many people the impression that all bears wander around the woods dreaming of noodle soup and chocolate bars. They don't. Still, any new or interesting odor can attract a naturally curious bear, and the big problem is that while there may be a few places in Alaska and Canada where bears have never tasted human food, you have to assume the worst. Operate on the principle that most bears in North America associate humans with food. You can't lose with this approach. If you're visiting a place where bears are food-conditioned, proper food storage techniques will protect your precious food cache from hungry, inquisitive bears. If the bears in your area have never sampled human food, yours won't be the first, and you won't be responsible for the death of a bear or a human injury. Remember: Once bears get food from humans, they're addicts, and most addicts die young.

COOKING

Don't Cook—Eat Cold Food

If a bubbling pot of Coq au Vin smells good to you, imagine how interesting it smells to every bear near your camp. There's an easy way to eliminate cooking odors, greatly reduce food storage problems, and just make life afield simpler: Eat cold food. Most of us are lucky to get away for weekend or overnight hikes, and a day or two of dried fruit and granola won't compromise an enjoyable getaway. In *Wilderness Camping,* Denton W. Crocker tells of eating a steady diet of cold food for almost two weeks. He didn't get ridiculously tired of his cold food diet, and he found the freedom from pots and pans and cooking and cleaning to be quite liberating. He watched sunsets rather than washing dishes. Eating cold food is the easiest, most effective, and most commonly overlooked method of reducing food odors. It's not for everyone, though—hot chocolate and hot soup are far more satisfying on a cold, wet day than dehydrated prunes—but it really does help minimize the potential for food-related problems in bear country.

If You Do Cook...

Although many people think the main reason behind proper food storage is that you don't want a bear sniffing around your food cache at night, bears have walked into camps while hikers were cooking meals. In open country like the Arctic National Wildlife Refuge, cook in a location where visibility is good. This gives you time to react if you see a bear approaching. Before you start cooking, take a look around and ask yourself, What's the plan if a bear comes into camp? If you keep a large resealable plastic bag near your cooksite, it's handy for storing bits of food and trash that might otherwise hit the ground, and you could dump a hot, half-cooked meal into it if necessary. Zip. Put it in your bear can or take it with you rather than allowing a bear to dine on it.

You need to prepare for cooking before you even set out on a trip. If you do a lot of winter camping, you'll have to cook in your tent and it will be permeated with food odors. A thorough washing before the summer season will remove some odors, but it's better to have a different tent that you have never cooked in for summer camping. You should also carefully plan food quantities before you leave home, so you don't have to store leftovers while in bear country.

Once you arrive at your campsite, you need to set it up properly. Your cooking area should be a minimum of 100 yards downwind from your sleeping area, but check local requirements for the proper distance. You'll also need to check locally for the correct arrangement for your food storage, cooking, and sleeping areas. Some parks require a triangular arrangement with your sleeping area on the point and your food storage and cooking areas at the base. Other parks advise campers to keep their sleeping area 100 yards or more from a combination cooking–food storage area. Remember that cool air tends to flow downslope at night, so store your food downwind and downslope. Sea kayakers in coastal waters should cook below the high tide line, and wash their pots, dishes, and utensils by the shore in saltwater.

Once you begin preparing your meal, the following pointers should be kept in mind:

- Whether you're cooking along the coast of the ocean or a high mountain meadow, keep an open resealable plastic bag near your stove. This will help you resist the temptation of flicking small bits of food on the ground.
- Try to cook your evening meal in one location a few hours before dark. After eating, move on to the place where you plan to sleep.
- Cooking can be a chaotic affair, with spices here, soy sauce there, your main dish on the stove, and other food scattered everywhere. Once you're ready to start cooking, get all your food together in one place so you can grab it quickly if a bear ambles into the kitchen. Only take out the food that's needed. Don't eat picnic-style.

- Avoid bacon, sausage, fish, and other smelly food. In addition to giving off strong odors while cooking, the smell permeates your clothing.
- Never leave cooking food unattended.
- At home, we're all well-mannered people so we don't wipe our hands on our pants while we're cooking and eating. That's what washcloths and napkins are for, right? When we're camping, our Emily Post etiquette sometimes lapses. It's not a good idea to wipe your hands or—gasp—kitchen utensils on your clothes when you're camping in bear country. Keep a handkerchief handy for wiping your hands.

After you're done cooking, wash dishes immediately after each use. If there are a lot of food particles in the dishwater, dispose of it properly at least 100 yards from camp. Wash your hands and face thoroughly after meals and before going to sleep. Don't wash yourself or your dishes in freshwater lakes or streams.

Don't sleep in the same clothes you wore while cooking. Hang your cooking clothes in plastic bags. Food odors tend to permeate clothes, so you might want to smoke them over a fistful of sage, pine, or some other aromatic plant. Rinse out your handkerchief or dishrag and store it with your food and garbage.

FOOD STORAGE

When you store food, it might pay to make a game of it and pretend you're playing keep-away from Yosemite's intelligent and well-educated black bears. In Yosemite, some people use the counterbalance method of hanging food way out on a skinny tree limb that won't support the weight of an adult bear. It doesn't always work. People have witnessed bears get as close as they can and then make a flying leap at their food sack. In another case, people parked their classic Volkswagen bug at a trailhead, rolled the windows up tight, and locked it before going for a day hike. While they were hiking, a bear climbed up on the Volkswagen's roof and hopped up and down a few times until air pressure popped open the doors. If you can prevent a Yosemite bear from getting your food, you can probably foil any bear.

First, study the land and pick a food storage site that's not attractive to bears. Don't store food right beside trails, on the edge of a meadow, or near berry patches or other obvious sources of food. Try to pick a place that's in the open so you can examine it from a safe distance. I like to be able to see my food cache from my tent.

Once you've selected a good site, don't make the same mistake that has resulted in many dead bears and injured hunters. They kill an elk late in the evening, but, with darkness approaching, there's no time to quarter it and pack it back to camp, so they just gut it and hang the whole carcass from a tree. When they return to collect "their" trophy the next morning, they casually walk into a grizzly bear that fed on the gut pile at night. Charge. Bang. Injured hunter, dead bear.

Don't be a yahoo. Before you begin walking toward your food cache in the morning, use binoculars to examine it. Study the surrounding area for bears. Take a few minutes. Look for ravens and other scavengers that might suggest your food has been strewn around. Don't make your approach until you're certain there are no bears around, and make a bit of noise just to be sure.

Here are a few examples of food, garbage, and odorous items used for preparing and/or eating food that must be properly stored whenever they're not in use.

- All human food
- Fresh fish

Some bears regard ice chests as bear feeders, so when you park your car at a trailhead, keep ice chests and all other food and beverage containers hidden from sight.

- Wine, beer, soda: any full or empty beverage can
- Water bottles that contained drink mixes and all plastic bottles
- Stoves and fuel
- Ice chests, silverware, cooking utensils
- Cooking clothes
- Lotions, ointments, sunscreens, and all other toiletries
- Soap, shampoo, medications
- Horse and dog feed
- Trash and garbage

And what about your pack? Whenever possible, I try to hang my pack. I'm always concerned that carrying food in the pack somehow left food odors in it. I once had ground squirrels in Glacier Park chew apart my salty, sweat-soaked shoulder straps. If you can't hang your pack, don't bring it in your tent at night. Unzip all the pockets, empty them, leave them open, and leave your pack outside the tent.

Food Storage Equipment

Whoever invented resealable plastic bags did the backpacking community a big favor, and I couldn't survive in the backcountry without garbage bags. The dry bags used by kayakers and canoeists are much sturdier than garbage bags, and bear-resistant food containers are the ultimate food storage device. You'll need light rope or parachute cord for hanging your food from trees. When people think about food storage, they're usually wondering how they can keep their food safe at night. Remember that you need to keep food and food odors away from your clothing, tent, and pack, too. That's why resealable plastic bags and garbage bags are so handy.

Bear-resistant food containers are heavy-duty ABS plastic cylinders about the size and shape of a summer sleeping bag in a stuff sack. People who use them regularly just call them bear cans. They're about 18 inches long by 8 inches in diameter. Bears can't get their jaws around them or undo the lids, which are secured with two flathead screws that fit flush with the surface of the container. You can tighten the screws with a coin, a knife, or whatever's handy. Bear cans are sleek, smooth, and damn near indestructible. The manufacturers can't say they're bear-proof—that's an invitation for a lawsuit—but until bears learn how to use Swiss army knives, a properly secured bear can will prevent grizzlies or black bears from getting at the food inside. They make good camp stools, too. That's the good news.

The bad news is that bear cans are heavy, clumsy, clunky things with a relatively small storage capacity. Rectangular blocks of cheese or even those square little vegetable bouillon cubes just weren't designed to fit into a perfectly round cylinder. You have to mash food into bear cans. Even then, you always waste a bit of space.

Because bear cans are big and heavy, they don't ride well when strapped to the outside of a pack. Try to put them inside your pack, and strap lightweight, bulky items on the outside. It's usually easy to get a bear can into the hatch of a sea kayak, but sometimes you have to leave a bit of space inside the hold, maneuver the bear can in, and then pack around it. Bear cans don't float, and they're not watertight, so store them upside down so rain doesn't leak in. Don't use them as a stand for your stove, because they'll melt. Bears can't break them, but you can—the tabs are the weak spot. It's easy to break the tabs off the lid. You can buy or make a nylon carrying case with an assortment of buckles and D-rings that allow you to strap the containers on the outside of your pack or vessel. The carrying case also gives you a means of hanging the container from trees, a requirement in some parks, forests, and recreation areas.

Bear cans are not only heavy and ungainly, they're expensive. Despite the cost, size, and weight of bear cans, they have one redeeming quality—they work. They really work. After the National Park Service began requiring backpackers to use bear cans in Denali in 1984, there was a 95 percent reduction in bears obtaining food from backpackers and an 88 percent decrease in property damage in the backcountry. If you want to reduce food odors that might attract bears, prevent bears from getting into your food, and reduce the odds that you'll have a bear in camp at night, use a bear can.

Hanging Food, Garbage, and Odorous Items

As a general rule, your food should be hung at least 10 feet off the ground and 4 feet away from the tree trunk, but check local requirements. In some parks and forests, hanging your food out of reach of bears is easy: use the cables, crossbars, or food poles generously provided by agencies such as the Park Service and Forest Service. Don't tie off your rope or cord on support poles because bears will sometimes climb those poles, bump the rope, see your food bag move, and make the connection.

If you're on your own, the counterbalance technique is the best method for hanging your food from a tree. In Yosemite, it merely forestalls the inevitable, but it will foil bears almost anywhere else. The idea is to hang two food sacks of equal weight way out on a tree branch where bears can't reach them. The main problem with the counterbalance technique is finding the right tree with the right branch. Your first requirement is a "live" branch at least 15 feet above the ground. The branch must be strong enough to support the weight of your food but not sturdy enough for a bear cub to walk on. You're looking for a branch about 4 to 5 inches in diameter at the base and only 1 inch in diameter at the point where you hang your food.

With the counterbalance method, your food must be at least 10 feet above the ground and 10 feet away from the tree trunk. You want your food sacks to hang about 5 feet below the branch.

1. Begin by putting a rock or weight of some sort in a sock, tying a rope to it, and throwing it over the branch. Move the rope as far out toward the end of the branch as possible. Some manufacturers now make "bear bags" with a food sack on one end of the cord, and a smaller sack to hold a weight at the other end. Thick rope is less likely to tangle. Wearing gloves will prevent rope burns

2. Your food should be in two sacks or containers of equal weight. They shouldn't weigh more than 10 pounds each because an inch-thick branch won't support more than 20 pounds.

3. Tie one end of the rope around the neck of one sack, securing it firmly. Tie a loop in the rope near your sack for retrieving your food later. Hoist the sack all the way up to the branch by pulling

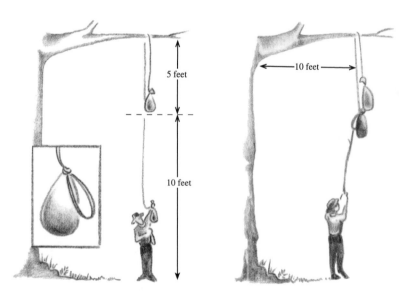

Counterbalance food hanging method

on the free end of the rope. Now reach up and tie your second food sack as high up on the rope as you can. Again, tie a secure loop in the rope near the second sack. Put any excess rope into the sack.

4. Toss the sack into position or push it up with a stick so the sacks are balanced over the branch. Don't forget: A 6-foot-tall person will need a 5- to-6-foot-long stick to hook the loop on the food sacks when it's time to retrieve them.

Properly executed, this technique will foil most bears, raccoons, and other late night raiders—but it's not bear-proof in places like Yosemite. It will buy you time, that's all. If you're lucky, you'll hear the bear(s) and have time to get out of your sleeping bag and take action before your food is gone.

You can also suspend a food bag on a rope strung between two trees conveniently located about 23 feet apart. You'll need 100 feet or more of ⅛-inch or larger nylon rope, a weight of some sort for throwing the rope over tree limbs, and a carabiner or short piece of nylon cord for attaching your food sack to the rope.

1. Throw the weighted end of your rope over a limb about 17 feet high. Lower the weight to the ground. Tie off the other end of the line as high up as you can reach on the base of tree No. 1.

2. Now pull all your slack over the limb, run the rope along the ground toward tree No. 2, and set your food sack on the rope a little more than halfway between tree No. 1 and tree No. 2. Then throw the weighted end of the rope over a 17-foot-high limb on tree No. 2.

3. Attach your food bag so it will be in the middle of the line between the trees.

4. Hoist up your food bag and tie off the rope on tree No. 2. The food should be about 12 feet above the ground.

This system is fairly effective with novice bears. Experienced food robbers will wonder why you didn't set up a table with silverware for them. They'll simply rip off the line from the tree trunk and feast on your food when it falls down.

One last technique is to throw a line over a limb, suspend your food 12 feet above ground and 5 feet below the limb, and then tie the line off as high up on the tree trunk as you can reach. This technique is better than nothing with inexperienced bears, and it helps keep mice, squirrels, and other pests out of your food.

When your food is 12 feet high, wind will disperse the scent more than if it were on the ground. Keep your food in plastic bags to reduce odors.

Hanging food from tree branches can test your patience. It's easy to draw an illustration showing the perfect branch, but finding one in the field is another matter. You settle for a branch that looks right, but a tangle of other branches is in the way. Your aim is a little off and you're snagged on the wrong branch. You try again and this toss falls short. Then you hit the branch. Curses. When you finally manage to toss your rope over a limb, it's too close to the tree trunk and little nubs on the limb prevent you from moving the rope out where it should be. Reading step-by-step instructions for hanging food is far easier than doing it in the field; however, you need to be as persistent as the bears that might try getting your food.

Storing Food on the Ground

If you're camping above timberline or exploring remote, treeless areas of Alaska and Canada where you have no choice but to store your food on the ground, I recommend using bear cans whenever possible. I know, I know—bear cans are too big and bulky and heavy. You can't fit enough food inside for extended trips. Sorry, a generation of hikers in Denali National Park has found ways to fit their food in bear cans and you can, too. Remember—before Denali National Park started requiring the use of bear cans, bears often found food that was cached on the ground in plastic bags.

What if bear cans are wholly impractical? Let's say you're taking a three-week hike in the Arctic National Wildlife Refuge. Bring the least odorous foods practical, double-bag everything, and then stash it at least 100 yards from your tent in a spot you can see. Avoid trails and areas where there are bear foods. Biologist Steve Herrero says he would never "sleep with my food to protect it. I would rather lose the food than risk injury."[3] I agree.

One writer suggests keeping your precious food "within bear-spray distance of your camp."[4] I wouldn't. Bears have been known to investigate camps at night. A bear might just grab your whole food cache and move away from your tent to dine in peace. For the rest of its life, that bear would investigate every camp it came upon in hope of finding another food reward. If a bear chose to eat your food where she found it, she might decide to check out your tent next. If you woke up because you heard the bear eating your food, would you have the moxie to get out of your sleeping bag, grab your pepper spray, unzip your tent door, and spray the bear? Even if you succeeded in driving off the bear, I suspect the food reward it attained would encourage it to investigate other camps.

You could also put food in dry bags and submerge them by weighting them with a few rocks. Just be sure to look along the shore for bear trails and make sure the water is fairly deep. Every summer hikers in Yellowstone put six-packs of beer and soda in creeks to cool it, and every summer bears find it.[5] If there are cliffs or big boulders nearby, it might be possible to hang your food bag out of reach. However, bears are much better at scaling cliffs than the average person is. You'd have to be a skilled rock climber to reach places a bear can't. Try to put your food in a place that's visible from your tent—if you happen to notice wolves, foxes, or other curious critters investigating your cache, you can frighten them away.

Food Storage While Car Camping

Sometimes we find ourselves spending the night in a car campground by a trailhead or using a car campground as a base camp for exploring a national forest or park. You have to be extra careful at car campgrounds in bear country. They're often situated in prime bear habitat. As a generalization, car campers tend to have a cavalier attitude about bears. They leave out ice chests filled with food. They spill food on picnic tables and don't clean it up. All too often people have allowed bears to obtain food here in the past, so food-conditioned bears might visit the campground again. If the campground's garbage cans are overflowing, or if the garbage cans aren't bear-proof, you should consider camping somewhere else.

Parks such as Yosemite provide bear-proof metal storage boxes/lockers and bear-proof garbage cans. Use them. An alarming number of people don't. If bear-proof metal storage boxes are not available, put all food and related supplies in the trunk of your car. Some bears know that ice chests and tin cans contain food, so don't tempt a bear by leaving them in plain sight on the back seat of your car. If your vehicle doesn't have a trunk, cover all food and food-related items with a blanket or something so bears can't see them. Keep your windows tightly closed. If you crack open your window even a quarter of an inch, bears can hook their claws inside and pull out the window. Lock your doors. Bears can easily rip down window frames to get at food they see inside your car. They pry and push and pull to test the strength of any edge or corner they can get a grip on.

When it's practical, seal food in air-tight containers or plastic bags to minimize odors. Never leave your camp unattended if food is not stored safely. Not all bears are nocturnal raiders; some bears make daytime forays into camps. Store your food properly day and night. Put your trash in bear-proof dumpsters and garbage cans frequently. Keep a clean camp.

As you're driving through Yellowstone, you might find yourself stuck in what appears to be an old-fashioned "bear jam." However, today's bear jams are different from the bear jams of the past. "Don't feed the bears" regulations are strictly enforced. No hot dogs, candy bars, or potato chips for the bears. No artificial food.

But there's plenty of natural food for bears along the park's roads, and that's why park officials have made the bold move of allowing bears and people to co-exist in fairly close quarters. "A bear repeatedly exposed to humans at close range without negative experience learns to tolerate them at these distances," states the *Staying Safe in Bear Country* video. "This is called human-habituation, but does not mean such a bear is tame."

Habituated roadside bears probably won't show any apparent concern about your presence, but don't take this as an invitation to approach. "A bear's personal space shrinks as it's habituated," says the *Staying Safe in Bear Country* video, "but it's still there. To crowd in can be dangerous."

To protect bears and people in Yellowstone, here are a few pointers:

- Stay in your vehicle. Do your viewing and photography through a window.
- The best way to get closer to a bear is with binoculars or a spotting scope.
- If you choose to leave the safety of your vehicle, stay nearby so you can get back inside quickly if a bear approaches. Remember that it's illegal to approach within 100 yards of a bear. It's best to not approach bears at all. Walking closer and closer to a bear stresses the animal and you're just asking for trouble. Eventually you'll enter the bear's personal space and force it to fight or flee. Let the bears dine in peace.
- Don't throw rocks or any other objects to get a bear to look up.
- If a bear decides to cross the road, let it through. Don't try to block its travel route.
- Don't run or make sudden movements.
- Be extra careful with your children.
- Don't feed the bears, and don't leave behind treats.
- Be aware that during a bear jam, crazy drivers are probably the greatest danger. "Honey, what are all those people looking at?" Bam.

Rangers in Yellowstone are usually quick to arrive at bear jams to make sure people behave. Outside the park, the roadside bear situation is not as well monitored, and bears are paying the price. One trouble spot is the North Fork of the Shoshone River, which runs along the highway from Cody, Wyoming to Yellowstone's East Entrance. In 2003, an orphaned 3-year-old grizzly was killed because people had been seen feeding him. The bear would approach vehicles in hope of getting a handout. "The same story happens year in, year out on the North Fork," said Mark Bruscino, bear management officer with the Wyoming Game and Fish Department. "People think it's fun to feed them."[6]

It's a growing problem throughout the West, where a maze of highways, gravel roads, and logging roads in bear habitat is bringing people and bears together with increasing frequency. Initially, it's natural food that attracts bears. You can't blame the bears for trying to utilize prime bear habitat. Then people feed the bears, and bears die.

You don't have to be one of those people; the onus is on you to behave ethically. The best thing to do if you spot a roadside bear is to drive by. Outside of Yellowstone, roadside bears have a high death rate. They get into unsecured garbage and food. They're more likely to be killed by hunters. They're susceptible to poachers. But if you can't resist stopping for a roadside bear, follow the guidelines above.

Human-habituated roadside bears are not necessarily a problem. Add food to the equation, and you've got problems. A fed bear is a dead bear.

Food Storage While Boating

You should always think of a beach as a bear trail and assume that bears will investigate anything you leave on the trail. Tracks on the beach have shown me that bears will make a big detour to check out a kayak dragged ashore above the high tide line. Don't tempt curious bears by leaving food in your kayak or stored beneath your canoe. There's a chance the bear will casually rip apart your kayak to get at a bag of dried fruit you accidentally left behind your seat. They can flip your canoe over like it's a toy. Once you're on shore, keep food away from your canoe or kayak to minimize the risk that a bear will damage it.

GARBAGE

Pack it in, pack it out. Make it easy on yourself by eliminating useless packaging material when you pack for your trip. Never bury garbage. Bears will smell it and dig it up. If campfires are allowed and you attempt to burn garbage, you'll still have to dig every charred scrap of food and

Bears will damage a kayak or canoe to find food stored in or beneath it.

aluminum foil out of the ashes and pack it out. Don't take any chances. You can never be certain that complete combustion has destroyed every trace of food and food odors. The packaging for hot chocolate, instant soup, and freeze-dried food does not burn completely. Some heavily used backcountry areas have pit toilets; don't throw any food or garbage in pit toilets because bears might tip them over to get the food, and in your next life you'll be given the duty of cleaning up the mess.

BREAKING THE RULES

I've come across two books and one magazine article that advise people to violate food storage rules. Their message is: Don't bother with the whole rigmarole of hanging your food from a tree—just put it in a garbage bag and cache it on the ground a good, safe distance from your campsite.

I object. The rationale for breaking the rules is that in popular places like Minnesota's Boundary Waters Canoe Area bears constantly check out campsites. Many campsites have only one really good tree for hanging food, and the bears know where it is. If you don't hang your food just right, bears will get it. Even if you do hang your food properly, you might find out the hard way that the tree branch you selected was actually less than perfect. To outsmart camp bears, don't put your food where everyone else does. Instead, put odor-free food in plastic bags and stash them on the ground well away from your campsite, game paths, and hiking trails.

After giving you this advice, the authors go on to say that in twenty years of camping they've never had a bear get into their food. I believe them. But what would happen if the Forest Service told every camper in the Boundary Waters Canoe Area, "Forget about hanging your food from trees. Use Joe Rebel's time-proven food storage techniques."

My guess is that by the end of one season, there would be a well-established path leading from each campsite to the "secret spot" where 90 percent of all campers hid their food. Bears would figure out the system and follow the path to the campers' food. Just because you tell people to store their food 100 yards or more from camp doesn't mean they're going to do it. (Remember that only 3 percent of Yosemite's backcountry users stored their food properly.) Human nature being what it is, a lot of people camping in the Boundary Waters Canoe Area would throw their food on the ground 50 or 25 yards from camp. Before long, bears would figure out that a methodical search within 50 yards of any campsite would probably lead to a bag of goodies. When grizzlies hunt elk calves in Yellowstone, cow elk try to lead the bear away while their almost scentless calves lie still on the ground. Some grizzlies ignore the cows and conduct a grid-like search for the calves.[7]

In the unlikely event that every camping party of the summer did walk off in a different direction to store their food, all the brush, shrubs, and trees around the campsite would be trampled. From the air, every campsite would look like a bomb crater. Joe Rebel's time-proven food storage techniques might work for one person, but as a public policy it would be a disaster.

The agencies are in a tough position. Once the decision is made to allow large numbers of people to camp overnight in bear country, food storage is a critical issue. Joe Rebel's food storage plan won't work. Yet finding the perfect tree to hang food is difficult. Yellowstone Park has installed bear poles for hanging food at backcountry campsites. They detract from the wilderness. You hike for miles to get away from cars and buildings and human artifacts, and when you arrive at your campsite—yuck—there's this ugly-bear pole. Park administrators don't like paying for them and backcountry rangers don't like looking at them any more than you or I, but what are the alternatives? Bear cans are one solution and are required in Denali and other parks. If you've got a better idea for storing food than the current system, land management agencies would love to hear about it.

Always think of the big picture when confronted with burdensome food storage regulations. I believe the situation we now have in places like the Boundary Waters Canoe Area or the Bob Marshall Wilderness Area is analogous to Yellowstone in the 1950s. Back then, beggar bears were a regular feature along the roadside. They also rummaged through the campgrounds. The National Park Service installed bear-proof garbage cans and launched an intensive educational campaign. Bears promptly began looking for food in hotels, campgrounds, and other developed areas. Dozens, some say hundreds, of bears were killed, but eventually people stopped feeding bears. The mama bears that survived were no longer rewarded for visiting campgrounds, so they stopped going and their cubs never picked up this habit. Now bears no longer associate the roads or campgrounds with food. It takes at least a generation or two for efforts like this to succeed. It takes constant vigilance, because in years when natural foods are scarce, even bears that have never tasted human food before are more likely to check out campgrounds and other human settlements for food. In the long run, proper food storage makes the woods a better place for bears and us.

Camping and Travel Tips

CAMPING

Campsite selection is critically important. Some campsites where people have traditionally preferred to pitch their tents—lakeshores, stream bottoms, on the edge of alpine meadows—are places bears prefer, as well. People like these campsites because they're on or near trails, and for the convenience of nearby water. Bears like these places because they're on or near trails, and for the convenience of nearby food. If you're in mountainous country, don't camp on saddles or ridges that are gentle enough to serve as natural travel corridors. Where forests and meadows meet, bears tend to stick to the edge of the meadow or travel just inside the cover of the forest. These are bad places to camp. You're better off deep in the forest or way out in the open. Don't pitch your tent where bears feed, rest, or travel regularly.

In some parks you don't get to choose your campsite—backcountry users in Yellowstone and some other parks are required to stay in designated sites. Beware. These sites were not selected with bears in mind. The National Park Service simply made traditional campsites (some dating from the 1870s) into designated sites. Traditionally, people have camped in all the wrong places.

If you're not familiar with the country where you'll be camping, take a good look at a topographic map and ask questions. How far back is my campsite from the lakeshore? How close am I to that stream? Are

Choose campsites carefully. The places people prefer are often the same places bears prefer.

there any spawning fish in the stream? After studying a topographic map and asking a few pointed questions, you might decide to select a different campsite.

When you camp in a designated site, you risk paying for the sins of others who camped there before you. Did they spill food when they were cooking fish over an open fire? Did they lose a tube of toothpaste that was later discovered by a bear that now pays regular visits to your designated site? You might see digging or other evidence that a bear has visited this camp. You might not. Usually, there's no way of knowing.

The good news about designated sites is that some are equipped with bear poles, food storage lockers, or cables for hanging your food safely from a tree. This reduces the risk that a bear visited your site and was rewarded with food.

Set up camp well before dark so you're not forced to pitch your tent in a bad location just because you ran out of daylight. Bears use hiking trails at night, so don't set up camp right next to a main thoroughfare. Coastal kayakers should avoid a narrow beach backed by cliffs or a high, steep slope. A bear walking along the shore would be funneled right through your camp. Stay a couple hundred feet away from streams as well as from the meadows and beach flats near freshwater streams. Spawning fish may attract bears to these areas, and the gurgling water makes it difficult to hear. You can often see bad campsites from the water.

If others who camped before you have spilled food, you might be visited by a bear that now pays regular visits to the site.

FACT OR FALLACY ?

FALLACY
The National Park Service carefully considers the bear situation before designating back-country campsites.[1]

FACT
In the October, 1990 issue of *Backpacker,* Doug Peacock wrote, "Government agencies usually mandate that you camp at established sites often located in drainage bottoms, lakes, or in open areas traditionally selected because of the great scenery. These are places bears frequent as well."[2]

For a good campsite, look for a wide beach. The forest behind it should be flat or have a gentle uphill slope. Scout the area before setting up camp. Sometimes there are game trails just inside the forest. Bear trails are much wider than deer trails. If you pitch your tent in an open area that's either in or adjacent to the beach zone, you'll have good visibility, and bears walking along the shore or just inside the forest won't walk right into your camp. If you decide to camp in the forest, go well back into the trees—100 yards or more. Don't camp right where the beach meets the shore because bears tend to walk in this transition zone.

Night Visitors

Bears typically check out campsites in the wee hours of the morning when everything is quiet. "At least three-fourths or more of the bears that enter camp do so from 2 a.m. to 5 a.m., the time when people are most quiet and sound asleep," says BYU professor Tom Smith.[4]

If you have enough space in your tent, sleep in the center and put your gear along the outside edges. A bear investigating your tent is likely to sniff, paw, and then bite—better to have it bite your hiking boots than bite your butt.

Some people encircle their camp with rope, parachute cord, or wire and dangle metal cups from the rope. If a bear bumps into your perimeter wire at night, the noise may alert you.

Better to have two people in two tents than four people in one tent. When you're split up, if a bear goes into one tent, there's sure to be a lot of noise and commotion, and people from the other tent can help drive the bear away.

BLEND IN

BYU professor Tom Smith researches brown bears in Alaska, while biologist Tom Beck studies black bears in Colorado. Over the years, both men have noticed that bears will "visually lock onto" people dressed in brightly colored clothes at distances up to a half-mile away.

When Beck set out camera traps to film bears, he baited the traps with odorous fish. He also protected delicate infrared transmitters for the cameras by mounting them in short sections of bright blue plastic pipe. Beck saw bears look at the pipe from a considerable distance, lose interest in what they'd been doing, and then move in to closer to check things out. At the camera site, bears were more interested in the novel color and shape of the pipe than the fish used for bait.

Tom Smith spends most of his summer based in a research camp on the coast of Katmai National Park, which boasts a dense population of brown bears. When Smith switched from bright blue and electric yellow tents to camouflage tents, bear visitation to his camp plummeted.

Combine bears' visual capabilities with their habit of checking out anything novel in their environment, and the lesson is clear—blend in so you don't become the object of a bear's curiosity. If you set up camp on a spot with a commanding view, you're offering bears coming from any direction a view of your tent. Bears notice brightly colored clothes and tents. To avoid attracting bears, or being detected by bears, blend in with camouflage or earth-tone colors. Don't stick out by camping on a ridge or high spot where the silhouette of your tent stands out; blend into the landscape.[3]

Sleeping under the stars is not a good idea in bear country. While there have been a few cases where bears pulled sleeping people from tents, there are more cases where bears attacked people sleeping under the stars. The flimsy nylon walls of a tent offer no physical protection against bears; however, bears tend to approach strange new objects cautiously. There's a chance you could wake up at night and hear a bear outside your tent. Predatory attacks by grizzlies occur most often at night; if this should happen, take action:

1. Fight the urge to quietly shrink down into your sleeping bag.
2. Talk softly to the bear so it can identify you as a human being.

3. If you have pepper spray, get it ready (see "Guns and Pepper Spray").
4. Pick up your flashlight, quickly unzip your tent door, turn on your flashlight, and shine it at the bear to momentarily blind it.
5. If the bear does not take off, whoop, holler, and make noise, or spray it with pepper spray if you have it.

Whether the bear is after you or your food, you want to get it out of there.

TRAVEL TIPS

Unlike grizzly bear mothers, black bear mothers seldom attack people in defense of cubs.... [R]esearchers who routinely capture cubs by chasing them up trees have not been attacked even when they have held screaming cubs. The ferocity of mother black bears is one of the biggest misconceptions about this species.
—Lynn L. Rogers, *Watchable Wildlife: The Black Bear*, 1992

The odds of being charged and injured by a black bear are remote unless you're a biologist working closely with bears or a ninny feeding roadside bears in a national park. *Staying Safe in Bear Country* notes that "[d]efensive attacks by black bears are very rare and the few recorded cases have been females defending their cubs." On the other hand, most skirmishes with grizzly bears occur when people inadvertently startle a grizzly at close range. It's often noted that, statistically, the odds of being killed while driving in a place like Yellowstone or Banff are far greater than the odds of being killed by a bear while hiking in the backcountry. This just proves the adage that statistics are meaningless. Few people lose any sleep over the thought of dying in a car wreck—we didn't evolve to fear this type of danger—but the idea of being attacked by a bear triggers an ancient and visceral fear in all of us.

A great deal of the advice that follows is intended specifically for people traveling in grizzly country, but some topics (like taking dogs afield) apply to both black and grizzly bears. However, even if you're never going to travel in grizzly country, you might want to take a look at both of the following sections.

GENERAL PRECAUTIONS
Dogs

Most bear literature tells you to leave your dog at home or keep it on a leash. The concern is that your dog will encounter a bear, get it all riled up, and then come running back to you with the bear in pursuit. The assumption is that you have an untrained, ill-mannered mutt. All too often that's an accurate assumption; however, some people have well-trained dogs that are an asset in bear country. These dogs can detect bears and warn you of their presence long before you'd know there was a bear about, especially at night.

Before you enter bear country with your dog, first check on local regulations. In many national parks, dogs are prohibited on trails and in the backcountry. Other places have leash laws. All land management agencies have different rules and regulations for different areas; be familiar with local requirements. Try to be realistic about your dog's training and behavior. There have been only a handful of incidents in which an off-leash dog provoked a bear attack, so the purpose of leash laws really isn't to protect you and your dog from bears. Instead, leash laws are meant to protect wildlife and other people from your dog. If you allow your untrained dog to run loose in the backcountry—especially backcountry areas with leash laws—expect confrontations with people who will be tempted to kick your dog and test-fire their pepper spray at its rude and inconsiderate owner.

Backpacks

Whether you're traveling in black bear or grizzly country, don't make the mistake of getting separated from your backpack. In places like Yosemite, some black bears have learned that packs often contain food. If you leave your backpack and walk off to take a photograph, a bear might get into your pack while you're gone. No matter where you are, don't give bears a chance to investigate your food and gear. In addition to the risk of losing your own food and gear, your mistake could corrupt a bear and teach it to investigate the gear of other people in the future. Carry your gear with you or stash it as carefully as you would when you set up camp for the night.

Islands

Bears are excellent swimmers, so whether you're kayaking along the coast of British Columbia or paddling in the Boundary Waters Canoe Area, be aware that, while small islands often have lower bear densities than other locations, they're not necessarily safe havens from bears.

GRIZZLY TIPS

If the fear of traveling in bear country is overpowering perhaps it is best that you travel on trails where there is little chance of encountering a bear. Ask at a ranger station or visitor center for their recommendations. There are numerous trails to visit in the Greater Yellowstone ecosystem. You have the luxury of choosing where to travel; the grizzly, due to limited habitat, does not.

—Yellowstone National Park, Beyond Road's End

Grizzlies hate surprises. Yellowstone Park wildlife biologist Kerry Gunther reviewed bear-related injuries in the park from 1980 to 1994 and found that eighteen of twenty-one injuries resulted from people surprising a grizzly in close quarters.[5] Don't surprise grizzlies and don't let them surprise you. I can't emphasize strongly enough that distance is a critical element when you're dealing with grizzlies. You don't want to step into a grizzly's personal space.

Be Aware. Fortunately, grizzlies and humans tend to avoid each other. If you pay attention to what you're doing, you will frequently notice grizzlies before they're aware of you. And grizzlies are aware of their surroundings enough that they often detect people before we're close enough to pose a threat. Contrary to popular belief, grizzlies don't want trouble. That's really what the statistics from Yellowstone tell us. Between 1980 and 1994 there were more than 600,000 visitor-use nights in the backcountry and thousands of people went for day hikes, yet there were only twenty-one grizzly-bear-related injuries. Grizzlies don't want trouble with you or with other bears—they want food. They generally avoid confrontations and fights.

One day at McNeil River, I saw a sub-adult male that was fishing for salmon on a gravel bar get sandwiched between a female with a spring cub 40 yards upstream and another big bear about 50 or 60 yards downstream. There was a steep bank thickly covered with alder behind the bears. Everything was fine until mama bear and her cub started walking toward the sub-adult's fishing hole. He watched them for a moment and then took a look downstream. Whoops. Trouble in every direction. The female and cub kept coming the sub-adult's way, so he clambered up the embankment. As mama bear walked downstream with her cub, I saw movement in the alders that showed the sub-adult was headed in the opposite direction. Mama bear stopped at his old fishing hole; moments later, the brush parted and he emerged at her former fishing hole. That's a typical bear encounter—at McNeil or any-where else. As biologist John Hechtel mentions in the *Staying Safe in Bear Country* video, "Bears do fight, but ritualized displays, avoidance and restraint characterize most interactions between bears."[6]

Just as grizzlies try to avoid confrontations with each other, they generally try to avoid us. Humans rely primarily on sight to detect grizzlies from a safe distance. Grizzlies depend on their nose but have good vision and hearing, too.

You'll often read that it's important to keep the wind at your back so bears can smell you coming, but that's usually not possible when you're hiking on a trail. You go where the trail leads regardless of wind direction. You should still pay attention to the wind, however. You need to be extra careful when the wind is in your face because then bears are less likely to hear you and won't be able to smell you. If the wind is blowing in the wrong direction, it negates the bear's best early warning system.

The fact that humans tend to believe what they see while bears have more faith in their sense of smell probably explains why we place so much emphasis on making noise in bear country. We can't "see" our smell drifting toward a bear, so we don't believe that bears can smell us. If they can't smell us and we can't see them, the only way to inform them of our whereabouts is to make noise. A lot of noise. So people wear bear bells. They travel in large groups and talk, talk, talk. They

Grizzlies stand on their hind legs so they can see, hear, and smell better. They lunge forward as they drop to the ground, which is often misinterpreted as a charge. Sometimes a bear will circle downwind to confirm with its nose what it has seen with its eyes.

have nonstop conversations that last for hours. They yodel or sing opera or blast boat horns. Some people insist that metallic sounds are the best way to alert bears of human presence because there are no metallic sounds in nature.

On the maze of trails that lace parks like Yellowstone and Jasper, there are so many people hiking through grizzly country that the amount of noise you make raises ethical and esthetic concerns. All the commotion displaces grizzlies from their preferred habitat. It ruins the tranquility for other hikers who came to the backcountry to escape the city's mechanical sounds. It disturbs bison, mountain goats, trumpeter swans, and other wildlife. Those critters don't have anywhere else to go. You do. If you're so nervous about grizzly bears that you have to make an excessive amount of noise, why not hike someplace where there are no grizzly bears?

Of course, the key word here is "excessive." What's excessive? Everyone has their own definition. You'll have to decide for yourself when you're afield.

Personally, I clap my hands or give a loud "hey Joe" when necessary. ("Hey Joe" is better than "Hey bear" because other hikers hearing "hey bear" might think you're yelling at a nearby bear.) I'd hike in a Scottish kilt and cowboy boots before I'd wear bear bells or walk with a group of people who talked nonstop for 8 hours straight. What would you talk about? The Internet? The World Series? Cosmetics? If you're walking through Jasper National Park's backcountry talking and thinking about politics, perhaps you should reconsider your whole approach to the wilderness.

My philosophy is to leave the urban world behind and focus outward. I strive to see or hear grizzlies before they're aware of me. I pay attention. I think about where I am and what I'm doing. As biologist Steve Herrero notes, "Your best weapon to minimize the risk of a bear attack is your brain."[7] I don't believe it's possible for your brain to simultaneously tune out the steady ring, ring, ringing of bear bells, talk about what you're going to have for dinner, and focus on your surroundings.

My friend Steve Fuller, a Yellowstone winterkeeper says he often notices train lines of noisy hikers while riding his horse in the backcountry, but they're not always aware of him. They're not paying attention. "Physically," says Fuller, "they've escaped the city and left behind the walls of their apartments and automobiles. But not mentally. They're alienated from the environment."

The kinds of hikers who don't spot a man sitting on a 1,000-pound horse aren't likely to see a 400-pound bear that's only 3 feet tall at the shoulders. They're operating on four dubious assumptions. One, it's the bear's responsibility to hear them coming. By making noise they've done their part; the rest is up to the bear. Two, bears will hear them coming. Three, a bear will leave when it hears them approaching. Four, it's all right to drive grizzlies away from their food and preferred habitat—not to mention disturbing other wildlife and hikers.

Instead of bludgeoning your way through the woods like Attila the Hiker, why not think of yourself as a guest in grizzly country, a polite visitor who doesn't want to disturb his or her hosts more than necessary? Make an effort to see or hear grizzlies before they notice you. Just as you can see better at night if you close your eyes tightly for a minute and then look around, you'll hear a lot better in the wilds if you begin your hike by getting away from the trailhead and then just sitting quietly for a few minutes and listening. Remember that urban noise is more than the sound of jets overhead and blaring car horns; the worries about work and relationships and other errant thoughts that clutter your brain are just noise and static that interfere with your ability to focus on the natural world you're about to enter. Try to clear your head before you enter bear country.

Bears can be noisy as they flip over rocks, rip apart decaying trees, and bash through thick brush. It's possible to hear grizzlies before you see them—if you aren't making a lot of racket yourself.

Don't make the mistake of expecting grizzlies to notice you. Sometimes bears are engrossed in feeding or playing. Sometimes they can't hear you approaching because of the wind or the noise of a stream. Sometimes bears have their heads up their posteriors. I doubt they're thinking about politics, but they're so preoccupied with some bearish thought they won't notice you.

I'm not saying you shouldn't make noise in grizzly country. There are times when it's necessary and appropriate. I just think you need to balance your concern for personal safety with your responsibilities to others.

Because my goal is to spot bears before they're aware of me, I consider binoculars an indispensable tool in grizzly country. I use them frequently. They help you spot bears when they're still a safe distance away. Binoculars allow you to see into dense timber and thick brush. Sometimes you'll hear a branch snap or notice a flash of movement. You might just see an unusual shape. With binoculars, you can pick out a patch of fur you'd miss with the naked eye. You watch and suddenly an elk will materialize. Or a grizzly.

When I worked as a fire lookout in northwest Montana, I learned to scan ridgelines for smoke. If there were a fire on a mountainside facing me, it was pretty obvious. If there were a fire on the other side of a ridge, all I'd see was smoke on the horizon. Scan the horizon in grizzly country. Check out the ridgelines and hilltops because you might see the hump of a grizzly or a halo of backlit hair.

It would be nice if enormous chocolate brown grizzlies always fed in bright green fields of 6-inch-tall sedge so we could easily see them, but it's more common to just see parts of a bear. You see a pair of rounded ears above the sagebrush and that's all. You peer into a patch of krummholtz in an alpine valley and notice the dish-shaped profile of a grizzly's head watching you. It helps to have a strong mental image of the animal. My wife is enchanted with rhinos, and when we're in Africa she inevitably sees them before I do. She's so keyed to rhinos that she easily picks out a rhino's horn in what looks like a tangle of brush and branches to me. Once I see the horn, the whole animal begins to take shape. Similarly, your first glimpse of a grizzly probably won't include the whole bear. It's more common to see part of the animal, one piece of the puzzle, before the whole bear becomes apparent to you.

When you're on the move during the day, choose your rest stops with care. Kayakers who pull ashore on the point of a peninsula will have a good view up and down the beach where bears might be walking. If you were to go just around the point, a bear could come around the corner and take you by surprise. When you make a rest stop, you need to consider visibility, wind direction, and all the other factors you take into account when selecting a campsite. Always try to rest, camp, or move so you have good visibility.

Use your binoculars to scan ridgelines and hilltops for bears.

NEVER RUN FROM A BEAR

"People who run from a bear can expect two things," according to biologist Tom Beck. "One, the bear will chase them and two, the bear will catch them."[8]

In BYU professor Tom Smith's database of Alaska bear attacks dating back to 1900, there are 42 accounts of people running from a bear. In 38 cases, the bear gave chase and injured the person.[9]

Chuck Neal gave a beautiful account of a bear's running ability in *Grizzlies in the Mist*. He spotted a grizzly feeding on a carcass in one of Yellowstone's sagebrush covered valleys. The bear sensed him. "The lone grizzly spun around in an upright position and hit the ground running. No one could have seen this bear run and entertain any illusions of outrunning a bear. The fleeing sub-adult ran away so fast from the carcass that, from my perspective, he seemed to be running, or rather floating, on top of the sagebrush for about 500 yards."[10]

I've seen grizzlies hunting newborn elk calves in sagebrush meadows; the spotted calves are well camouflaged and almost scent free so they hide on the ground and the bears make a grid-like search until they jump one. Once the chase is on, the bears' quickness and ability to turn on a dime is just as impressive as their speed. If you think you could outdodge a bear, forget it.

Travelers in grizzly country should watch and listen for ravens, magpies, coyotes, and other scavengers that could be feeding on the carcass of a moose or some other animal. There might be a grizzly nearby. Use your binoculars to scan at the base of avalanche chutes in the spring. If you notice a carcass while you're several hundred yards away, you can detour around it, but do so with care. Bears don't always camp right on top of the carcass. Sometimes they lay up in dense brush nearby.

In a paper on bear attacks, Steve French points out that a carcass may anchor a bear to a place for a few days.[11] If that place happens to be near a trail, the odds of people having a surprise encounter with a grizzly rise dramatically. The element of surprise combined with the bear's desire to protect its food has resulted in many deaths and injuries to people.

If you stumble upon a carcass (there may be a mound of dirt and branches piled on top of it), you're likely to stop and stare for a moment while your brain struggles to grasp the situation. Then you'll get a clear message: Uh oh. This could be bad.

A grizzly bear will often defend food like this elk carcass.

Don't run. Is the wind in your face or at your back? Take a look around. If you don't see a bear, the terrain and cover will dictate whether you should quietly move forward or back away in the same direction you came from. Chances are that if you came in this way undetected, you can leave the same way.

Another situation when you might inadvertently get close to a grizzly is by approaching a bear resting on a day bed. Grizzlies on day beds tend to be more tolerant of intruders than at other times—but that doesn't mean you want to push your luck. Pay attention if a trail takes you through an area that seems like a likely spot for bears to have day beds. Watch for krummholtz stands in alpine country, willow and alder thickets, dense tangles of timber, and downfall. Bears like moist sites on hot days. A grizzly will often scoop out a shallow dog-bed-sized depression at the base of a tree. As a rule of thumb, young bears tend to rest in areas with good visibility such as ridges, bluffs, and sandbars. Mature, dominant bears are more likely to bed down in dense brush. During windy weather, grizzlies spend more time than usual resting in day beds. The wind makes them skittish, as they can't smell or hear as well. Biologist Terry DeBruyn makes the same point about black bears in *Walking with Bears*. DeBruyn writes that bears "appear most ill at ease when the wind exceeds twenty miles per hour...they become uneasy, and unable to discern noises easily, they sit more often, looking about, testing the wind, and listening."[12]

TREE-CLIMBING RECONSIDERED

"If you decide to climb a tree, make sure you can reach the tree and get 15 feet up it before the bear gets there."

—Bill Schneider, *Bear Aware*[13]

When people have a sudden, close-up encounter with a black bear or a grizzly, there's a natural tendency to want to get away from the bear—fast. Maybe that's why some people make the mistake of trying to climb a tree to escape from a bear.

"Climbing a tree to escape a [black] bear is as bad as trying to out-run one," says biologist Tom Beck. "When bears fight, the loser often runs up the nearest tree to escape. Climbing a tree initiates the chase mechanism as surely as running."[14]

Biologist Stephen Stringham raised orphaned black bear cubs, and got to witness a friendly fight between siblings. Here he describes the action in *Beauty Within the Beast:* "Ontak leapt onto the trunk of a cotton-wood, sank his forepaw claws into its deeply fissured bark, and hopped upward. He was too slow. Jonjoanak arrived, raced up the tree after him, and bit into one of his heels. Hanging on with her teeth, she dragged her brother to the ground, where they sparred vigorously. This was all in fun, of course. But angry bears have dragged enemies, including people, out of trees the same way."[15]

Black bears are much better tree climbers than we are. They can quickly hoist themselves up limbless tree trunks most people couldn't possibly climb. Even if you manage to climb a little way up a tree before the bear catches you, now what? You're in a poor position to defend yourself. If you kick at the bear, it will just bite your foot or lower leg. In a discussion about bear attacks during the Fifth Western Black Bear Workshop, biologist Stephen Herrero noted that in five of nine cases where a female with young injured a person, "the female went up the tree after the person and pulled them out by the foot."[16]

In 1998, a Pennsylvania man came upon a female black bear and her cub feeding at a dumpster. He backed off and started climbing a tree. "The bear went after him, biting him from just above the knees down to his feet," reported Kathy Etling in *Bears and Other Top Predators.* "Basically, she bit the pants right off him. That might sound funny, but, when the bear finally left with her cubs, the man needed 325 stitches."[17]

(continued on next page)

(continued from previous page)

Don't trigger a black bear's chase mechanism by climbing a tree. Instead, stand your ground. Your body language will tell the bear, "touch me and it will cost you. I'm ready to defend myself."

If you don't notice a grizzly until it's charging, it's too late for tree climbing. The bear will be on you before you get to the tree. Stand your ground. If you just happen to be standing beneath the perfect climbing tree while a grizzly 47 yards away is making up its mind on whether to charge or flee, don't believe the myth that grizzlies can't climb trees.

It's true that adult grizzlies can't climb up a 12-foot-tall bare tree trunk like a squirrel, but neither can most hikers—even terrified hikers being pursued by a grizzly. If you can use tree limbs to climb a tree, a grizzly probably can, too. Grizzly bears chasing people up trees have "laddered" their way over 30 feet high.

Who says grizzlies can't climb trees? This isn't a fully mature grizzly, but even adult bears can ladder their way 30 feet up the right tree.

MAKING NOISE

Now let's discuss the topic of noise again, including sounds you shouldn't make. Don't whistle. Old-time Alaskans called marmots "whistlers." A grizzly will dig a ton of rock and gravel out of a mountainside to get one fat little marmot that gave a warning whistle and then dove into its den. Whistling in alpine bear country to move away grizzlies is like blowing on a predator call to frighten coyotes. If you're going to make noise in grizzly country, you don't want to sound like one of the great bear's prey species.

ARE BEAR BELLS EFFECTIVE?

Conventional wisdom says make noise to avoid surprise encounters with grizzly bears, and for years bear bells have been the noisemaker of choice. Bear bells are metal bells about an inch in diameter, and hikers attach them to their boots or pack and ding-ding-ding their way along the trail. It's often said that bear bells or any other metallic sound are the best way to alert bears of your presence because metallic sounds are unnatural. Bears are sure to notice metallic sounds.

When BYU professor Tom Smith tested this theory in Katmai National Park, the results took people by surprise. Smith attached bear bells to an alder beside a well-used bear trail. He tied fishing line to the alder, and ran the line 150 feet back to a blind where he could see bears on the trail. At first, Smith tugged on the line and tinkled the bells lightly—about the same noise level a hiker makes. Not one bear's ears perked up. Not one bear looked in the direction of the bells.

Smith then started really yanking on the line so the bells make a loud jangling noise. Fifteen bears waltzed by and ignored the jangling bells. Smith snapped a pencil, which sounds like a twig snapping. Bears turned and looked at his blind. He huffed like a bear. Bears on the trail looked his way.

These experiments should not be seen as irrefutable proof that bear bells don't work. This may well have been the first time some of Katmai's bears heard bear bells. They don't associate bear bells with humans, so it's possible they just tuned out the tinkling bells as background noise. On popular trails in more heavily visited parks like Jasper or Yellowstone, bear bells may be more effective at helping to prevent surprise encounters because bears have learned to associate the tinkling bells with people.

If you're going to tie bear bells to your pack or your bootlaces, be aware that bear bells aren't loud enough to be heard over rushing streams or on windy passes. Wearing bear bells is no guarantee that bears will always hear you coming. You can't rely on bear bells alone.

Clap your hands and give a loud "hey Joe" when you're coming to a blind corner on a trail. These are noises you always have with you. You can increase the volume and intensity as needed. Even a bad rendition of Jimi Hendrix's "Hey Joe" will help the bear identify you as a human.

Bear bells are not a particularly effective way to alert bears of your presence.

If you're hiking on a trail that follows along a noisy stream and thick vegetation limits your visibility, make noise. I make noise when I walk through waist-high patches of cow parsnip and other bear foods. I travel slowly. I stop and go, stop and go, carefully looking around each time I stop. I listen for bears. I don't just holler my fool head off. I never assume a bear will hear me, let alone that she's going to leave because she hears me.

Incidentally, when you first spot a bear, it's best to assume it's a female with cubs. Young bears don't always stick close to their mother, and, because cubs are small, they're tougher to see.

GROUP SIZE

One spring I got into a dangerous situation with a female grizzly and cubs while I was out on a photographic expedition with Doug and Lisa Peacock. We found a female with twins feeding in a meadow. We stashed our packs in a tree and then crept around until the wind was in our face and we were hidden in good cover. We knew we were well within the bear's personal space, but we were confident we could get photographs without being detected. We were wrong.

Our problems began when Doug ran out of film. He had a new camera and couldn't figure out how to open it to change the film. He is not a patient man. He was sweating and cursing softly while trying to pry the

!!#&8!! camera apart with his stubby little paws. The operating manual for his camera was in his pack. While Lisa tried to keep Douglas from roaring in frustration, I went back to the packs for the camera manual. This took me closer to the bears.

I'm sure Doug and Lisa assumed I was keeping my eye on the bears, but I lost sight of them momentarily while I was digging around in the pack. After I found the manual I looked around for the bears. I couldn't see them. I didn't hear anything. Ah, what the heck. I assumed that Doug or Lisa had been glancing up now and then to keep tabs on the bears. We all assumed wrong. Not one of us was paying attention the way we should have been. We were so close to mama bear that when she finally noticed us, she charged.

She swerved away before making contact, but it's still embarrassing to know we foolishly ruined the bears' peaceful day. We endangered ourselves and the bears. Looking back with 20/20 hindsight, we were too close, we should have kept our packs with us, and I should never have gone back toward the bears.

All of us had spent years hiking alone in grizzly country without making such a serious mistake, and whenever I read that you should always hike with a group because there's safety in numbers, I think about this incident. Three dolts are no safer in grizzly country than one bear-savvy person.

Statistically, however, solo hikers are at greater risk in grizzly country. People in groups of four or more are rarely injured by bears. There has never been injury to a group of six or more. There has never been a

FACT OR FALLACY ?

FALLACY
Bears growl to threaten nearby people.

FACT
Bears roar and make a variety of guttural sounds that most people interpret as growls, but reports of bears growling at biologists are rare. After spending six summers in close quarters with black bears, biologist Terry DeBruyn wrote that he never heard a bear growl. During a standoff with a nearby bruin, the bear might express its anxiety by popping its jaws (a hollow sound), salivating, or huffing. If it charges, the bear might roar. But there's only a remote possibility it will growl at you.

fatality in a group of four or more. BYU professor Tom Smith keeps a database on bear attacks in Alaska, and he "has no record of a bear that has charged and attacked two or more people standing their ground. 'As soon as you split up, you stack the odds against you," he says.[18]

This safety record stems from three factors. First, big groups of people tend to make more noise than smaller groups and are more likely to alert bears of their presence or drive grizzlies away. Second, large groups of people are more visible to bears. Grizzlies have a greater chance of seeing (or scenting) you in the distance and then moving away. Last, during an uncomfortably close encounter with people, grizzlies are less likely to conclude a rush or charge at a group of people than an individual.

Traveling with a group also comes into play when you're dealing with young bears that are curious and sometimes test people. A young bear that might approach one person on a beach along the coast of Alaska is far less likely to approach a group of people in the same situation. After years of leading groups of people among large numbers of bears at McNeil River, biologists have noticed that bears are more likely to approach a group of one to five people than a group of six to ten. If you go out alone at McNeil, you can almost count on a visit from a young, tolerant bear.

Steve French points out that it's easy for a group of hikers to get separated while hiking on a trail.[19] One person will forge ahead while another visits the bushes; the next thing you know, your group of six is widely spaced apart. When hiker No. 1 tops a ridge and bumps into a bear, the bear doesn't know that five other people are following. It sees one person, and that changes the dynamics of the encounter. You've lost all the advantages of hiking with a group.

Try not to get overconfident if you're hiking with a big group of friends. There's a tendency for each person to think the other person is taking care of business.

HIKING ROUTES

Many trails in grizzly country are unsafe by design. They were constructed decades ago without any consideration for your safety or the welfare of bears. They lead you through berry patches and meander through thick brush beside noisy streams. They follow along the edge of meadows and other natural travel routes for bears. They put you on a collision course with grizzlies. To make matters worse, trails allow people to hike at a fast pace. It's difficult to watch for bears (or other wildlife) while you're marching along at a steady 4 miles an hour.

Walking on trails allows your mind to wander when you should be paying attention.

Even in heavily used backcountry areas, it's not safe to assume that trails belong to people and the bears belong somewhere else. In Glacier Park, Montana, for example, some grizzly bears have learned to tolerate people on the popular Highline Trail. The bears use the Highline Trail both day and night. Despite the sheer number of people on the Highline Trail, the endless ringing of bear bells, and the endless prattle of inane conversations, you're far more likely to encounter a grizzly on this trail than on many other trails in Glacier. Habituated bears along trails are not often involved in altercations with hikers.

In Yellowstone, bear activity in late winter/early spring often occurs in geyser basins and thermal areas. That's where bears have the best prospects of finding edible vegetation. In addition, there might be winter-killed elk, moose, and buffalo. In Denali National Park, peavines are one of the few foods available to grizzlies in the spring.

The shape and texture of bear scat varies depending on what they've been eating. A diet of ripe berries produces runny piles of scat filled with seeds and half-digested berries.

They commonly grow on broad glacier river bottoms that are popular travel routes for hikers. If you're hiking along a river bottom in the spring, you really need to be on the lookout for grizzlies. Think about what kind of food a bear is most likely to be eating at any given time of year when you travel in grizzly country.

Grizzlies leave behind all sorts of signs. Their digging for roots and bulbs can look like somebody was using a Rototiller in a garden. They excavate large holes to dig out marmots and ground squirrels. Grizzlies roll over logs and flip over rocks to get at ladybugs and other insects. You will find grizzly tracks or scat if they're in the area.

I always pick apart bear scat to try and discover what the bruins have been eating. It's more than curiosity about their natural foods. I look carefully for bits of plastic and aluminum that tell me I should be prepared to contend with a food-conditioned bear that's been getting into garbage.

Don't cancel your hike just because you find bear signs. Unless you're looking at a steaming pile of half-digested berries or a quivering salmon carcass with bite marks on it, you'll have difficulty telling how long ago a grizzly was in the area. If it was an hour ago, the bear could easily be 5 miles away. Day-old bear sign in Canada's Waterton National Park might have been left by a grizzly that's now 20 miles away in the United States. The good thing about finding bear sign is it has a way of raising your level of bear consciousness.

Along the coast of British Columbia and Southeast Alaska, kayakers frequently pull ashore for rest stops near areas where both brown and black bears fish for salmon. Freshwater streams filled with spawning fish are an obvious place to watch for bears. It's common to have a shoreline with a strip of beach grass, then a wall of dense alder, and then a towering old-growth spruce forest. The beach grass can be tall enough to conceal either black or grizzly bears, and there are sometimes well-defined game trails just inside the spruce forest. If you're going to poke your head into the forest, you'll be momentarily disorientated and have trouble seeing because even on a typically overcast day along the coast, it's much brighter on the water and the beach than inside the cathedral-like forest. Give yourself a minute to adjust to your new surroundings before plunging into the forest.

Give grizzlies the right-of-way on trails or natural travel routes like beaches. That might seem self-evident, but there have been cases where hikers have provoked bears that weren't even aware of them. They shouted and waved their arms over their head in an effort to frighten the bear away from the trail. Instead, the bear charged or advanced toward them (usually just continuing along the trail). I think the problem stems from the overemphasis on making noise in grizzly country. Some people have blind faith in the idea that grizzlies will automatically run the other way if they hear you coming. That's not always true. In addition, some bear literature gives the impression that grizzlies understand trails are for humans during the day. Sorry, that's not true either. Grizzlies might habituate to people on trails or avoid trails, but they do not have any respect for proprietary rights you might feel for human trails.

TRAIL RUNNING IN BEAR COUNTRY

On the one hand, runners are covering ground faster than hikers... on the other hand, runners make more noise puffing and thumping through the woods... the thunder of size–10 Nikes might be enough to make some bears flee in panic."
—Craig Medred, "Bear Country Need not Be a Death Trap for Runners," *Anchorage Daily News*, June 11, 2006

In 1995, seventy-seven year old Marcie Trent and her forty-five year old son Larry Waldron went trail running in Alaska's Chugach State Park, which borders the city of Anchorage. They quickly separated, so it was Larry who ran into the grizzly first. The bear was feeding on a moose carcass beside the trail. It killed Waldron. A short time later his mother ran into the same bear, and met the same fate as her son. Evidently, their Nikes didn't "thunder" loud enough to cause the bear to flee in panic. Writing about the incident in *Mark of the Grizzly,* author Scott McMillion said, "Running in grizzly country can be dangerous: it can trigger a chase response in any predator, much like a cat chasing a ball."[20]

To the best of my knowledge, no bear has ever spotted someone running along a trail and given chase like a cat after a mouse. What makes trail running risky is the possibility of bumping into a nearby bear. You stop and stare in disbelief and the bear does, too. There's a possibility it will charge even though you're just standing there frozen with fear. Why? Because you've encroached on the bruin's personal space and forced it to make a hasty decision: fight or flee.

(continued on next page)

(continued from previous page)

UNDERSTANDING THE RISKS

"I always tell people trail running is dangerous."
—*Chugach State Park Ranger Jerry Lewanski*

"Bear Attacks Force Alaska Joggers to Find Safe Ways to Exercise" —*Christian Science Monitor*[21]

There are five reasons why runners in bear country tend to be at greater risk than hikers.

1. Hikers pay attention to their surroundings and watch for "bear-ish" situations. Runners pay attention to their feet.
2. Hikers often travel in groups of four or more. Runners go solo or get separated on the trail. A group of hikers generally talks and makes more noise than a solo runner.
3. Hikers yell and deliberately make noise when appropriate to avoid surprise encounters with bears. Thundering Nikes aside, runners move quietly.
4. Even if you startle a nearby grizzly, it will rarely conclude a charge if two or more people stick close together and don't move about. A solo runner is much more likely to be injured than two or more hikers.
5. Most hikers in grizzly country carry pepper spray; few runners do. Runners have no defense against a grizzly in a worst case scenario. That's easy to change. One company (UDAP) sells an 8 ounce can of pepper spray in a lightweight nylon holster designed so you can literally have pepper spray in the palm of your hand.

BEAR AVOIDANCE OF HUMANS

Most bears will avoid people and leave an area when they know people are present.
—Interagency Grizzly Bear Committee, *Grizzly Country,*
Bear Necessities: How to Avoid Bears

Bear literature constantly stresses that grizzlies "normally" avoid people; however, it's important to understand that avoidance occurs at two levels. It is normal for bears to avoid people and other bears in the sense that they don't want you inside their personal space.

Beyond that, the degree to which bears "normally" avoid people is debatable.

Nowadays, grizzlies often flee the moment they sense a nearby human. Is this normal? Historical accounts of the first meetings between Europeans and grizzlies no doubt exaggerate the ferocity of grizzlies; nevertheless, it's clear the bears weren't so quick to run away 200 years ago.

Let's not forget that shortly after the Lewis and Clark expedition killed thirty-seven grizzly bears on their journey to the Pacific, European settlers slaughtered millions of buffalo and began trapping and shooting bears to protect dull-witted domestic livestock. As settlement spread, ranchers introduced bears to the perils of strychnine, 1080, and other deadly poisons. In the 1960s, Alaska state employees—at the bequest of cattle ranchers on Kodiak Island—gunned down the biggest bears on earth from planes. During Alaska's pipeline days, construction workers fed bears dynamite sandwiches. In less than 200 years, we reduced the grizzly population in the continental United States from at least 50,000 bears to less than 1,000.

Humans slaughtered grizzlies with the fervor of a Hitler and the perversity of a Marquis de Sade. Little wonder the few surviving grizzlies have a tendency to avoid us. But we can only say bears normally avoid people if we're willing to say our behavior toward grizzlies during the past 200 years was normal. I'd like to think it was an aberration and that in the future we'll have the grace, the generosity of spirit, to accommodate grizzly bears.

Grizzlies don't always flee from humans, so if you spot a bear that's more than 100 yards away and not aware of you, don't immediately draw attention to yourself. Think about your situation. At that distance, you're not a threat to the bear. There's not much chance it's going to look up, see you, and charge because it feels threatened.

Whether you decide to take evasive actions or stay and watch the bear for awhile, you need to ask yourself a few questions. Which way is the wind blowing? Can the bear smell me? Can I slip away unseen when the grizzly drops down into a ravine 150 yards away? If it moves closer, what will I do?

If there's a route that simply allows you to avoid the bear, use it before the bear gets within 100 yards of you. If you can't get away undetected and the bear starts heading in your direction, I suggest that you alert the bear to your presence in a nonthreatening way when it's 100 to 150 yards away. Just clap your hands and say "hey Joe." If it seems inevitable that the bear will become aware of you, the farther away from you this occurs, the better. This gives the bear options.

It might leave. It might decide you're not a threat and keep going about its business. It may rush toward you, but, because of the distance, this action is more likely to be prompted by curiosity than fear. It may stop, stand on its hind legs, and try to smell or see you better. It might ignore you and keep feeding or doing whatever it was doing. Because the bear is now aware of you, it may only be pretending to ignore you—so leave. Once the bear is no longer moving toward you and is doing something besides looking at you, quarter away from it until you're a safe distance apart. By not moving directly away, you give the bear a better chance to see that you're a human; you don't give the bear the impression that its presence is the reason you're retreating. You can still keep an eye on the bear, but don't hang around. Don't risk another encounter with a bear you've already agitated once. Clear out of the area.

Mentally rehearse what you will do if a grizzly "pops up" unexpectedly.

Bears and Human Recreation

Even if you don't ride mountain bikes and even if you would never think of getting close enough to a bear to photograph it, you'll find in this chapter valuable tips that apply to all travelers in bear country, whatever their recreational pursuits. Here I focus on photography, fishing, mountain biking, and cross-country skiing.

PHOTOGRAPHY

> I never approach bears.
> —Tom Walker, *Outdoor Photographer*, March 1996

In the same 1996 issue of *Outdoor Photographer* in which Tom Walker emphasized that he never approaches bears, another prominent photographer said, "I never approach bears quickly and directly."[1]

The problem with s-l-o-w-l-y approaching a bear is that every person has his or her own definition of "slow," and I suspect every bear does, too. While a photographer who honestly believes he's slowly creeping toward a bear moves ever closer, the bear could be thinking, "If that fool sprints three more steps in my direction, I'm going to throttle him."

The one and only thing you can be sure of when you approach a bear is that you're going to put the animal on edge because it has no idea what your intentions are. Human behavior is truly unpredictable. The bear doesn't know whether you're friend or foe. One person wants a photograph; the other wants a bearskin to hang on the wall. When you approach a bear, eventually you'll encroach on its personal space, engage with the animal, and force it into "fight or flight" mode. This is true whether you're approaching a black bear beside the road in Great Smoky Mountains National Park, or a grizzly bear in the wilds of the Yukon.

Just as people traveling in bear country are usually more concerned about bumping into a grizzly bear than startling a black bear, the main safety concern of photographers is getting so close to a grizzly bear that they provoke a rush or a charge. The question photographers ask about taking pictures of grizzlies is, "How close is too close?" The answer is, "It depends."

Are you looking at a female with cubs or a solitary animal? Is the bear in heavy cover or is it in open country? Is it feeding in the vicinity of six other bears at a salmon stream on the coast of British Columbia or feasting alone in a subalpine meadow in Montana? Is it a female in estrus who's likely to attract testy male bears? Most important of all, what previous experience has this bear had with humans? Every situation is different, and every bear is an individual. There are hundreds of variables to consider, and some of them are unknowable. How could a photographer in Denali's backcountry know whether the bear she's looking at was eating garbage at a lodge in Kantishna the night before? It's best to leave yourself a big margin for safety.

Denali National Park requires backcountry users to stay a quarter mile (1,320 feet) away from bears. In *Bear Attacks: Their Causes and Avoidance,* Steve Herrero recommends 1,000 feet. At this distance, it's possible to get pictures of a bear in its natural surroundings if the light is right and you've got a long lens. At 1,000 feet, you're reasonably safe, and you won't cause undue stress or potential harm to the bear.

Some photographers ignore the ethics of stressing bears. They will push a bear until the bruin charges. They claim they can read bears so well, they'll even wait out charges based on an intuitive sense of what the bear will do, which is nonsense. When a nearby bear charges, what are your options? Run and the bear will give chase. Climb a tree and the bear will give chase and climb up after you if it doesn't catch you before you get to the tree. So your only option is to stand your ground.

PHOTOGRAPHERS—DON'T PLAY RUSSIAN ROULETTE WITH BEARS

"If you intend to photograph bears do so responsibly and allow the bear its space. Never pursue or intentionally approach a mother with cubs."

—*Bear vs. Man*

"I would always observe a bear at a distance to determine its mood and personality before approaching within camera range."

—*In the Path of the Grizzly*

Photographers who approach any bear are playing Russian roulette. Whether you approach a solitary male grizzly bear or a female black bear with cubs, you'll eventually cross a fluid and invisible boundary line marking the bear's personal space and force the bruin to fight or flee. Unless you're intimately familiar with the behavioral characteristics of the particular bear you're approaching, you don't know if you'll enter the bear's personal space at a distance of 160 yards, 91 yards, or 17 feet. It takes months of observation, not minutes, to learn the behavioral characteristics of an individual bear. Nobody—not even a biologist with years of experience studying bear behavior—can spend 10 minutes watching an unfamiliar black bear feed on dandelions and legitimately say, "That appears to be a mellow bear in a good mood. I'm sure she won't mind if I get a little closer for a picture."

Most photographers who approach bears have no idea when they'll enter the bear's personal space. Once they encroach on the bear's personal space, they don't know if the bruin will fight or flee. Should the bear charge, they have no idea if it will pull up five yards away, or put them in a hospital. Photographers who approach bears generally don't know what they're doing—they're playing Russian roulette with a bear.[2]

There's a good chance the charging bear will stop short because your body language says, "don't you dare touch me because I'm prepared to fight." The bear stops its charge short of making contact because of your behavior, not your !#**&! intuition.

What if you're visiting a place like Alaska's Arctic National Wildlife Refuge and you spot a bear 330 yards away that's feeding on berries and not aware of you? I'd say get out your binoculars, enjoy watching the bear, and follow Tom Walker's rule: Don't approach the bear.

Do take a look around and ask yourself what you're going to do if the bear comes closer. When are you going to let it know you're there? Will you be able to drop out of sight and move away when the bear is still a safe distance off? Do you have a good route for avoiding the bear? If you're comfortable with the situation, set up your gear and allow the bear to make the next move. This can get very dicey very quickly. One minute the bear is a reasonably safe 150 yards away and blissfully unaware of you; the next minute it's only 75 yards away. Suddenly the wind shifts. The bear scents you, rears up on its hind legs, and looks in your direction. Now what? (Help the bear locate and ID you as a human being with a loud "hey Joe." Slowly, not frantically, wave your hands overhead.)

I suspect a lot of people look at full-frame shots of bears in books and magazines and think, "Wow. The photographer must have been really close to that bear."

They probably were fairly close to the bear, but there aren't many places where it's practical or ethical to get very close to a bear. Any honest professional photographer will tell you that over 90 percent of the bear photos you see in various publications were taken from the road in Denali National Park or at bear-viewing areas like McNeil River or the Brooks River falls in Katmai National Park. When there's a female grizzly with a cub hanging around the road at Sable Pass in Denali National Park during the third week in July, the five professional photographers lucky enough to have a permit to travel on the park road that particular week will take thousands of pictures of those bears. Some of them will appear in national publications. So many photographers visit McNeil River that after twenty-one years as the Alaska Department of Fish and Game's manager at McNeil River, Larry Aumiller can flip through an article about bears in *Audubon* or *National Wildlife* magazine and name many of the bears in the photographs. More and more people are shooting pictures of captive bears. A trainer taps the bear on the end of its nose, the bear snarls, and—voilà—you've got a cover photo for a magazine taken from so close-up you can see cavities in the bear's teeth.

If you're trying to photograph bears in the wild, your goal should be to take pictures without having the bear know you're there. This means keeping some distance away, at least initially. In situations when that's not possible, say when a bear that's 200 yards away is aware of you, then you could allow the bear to willingly approach you. Sure it might be safe for you to move a little closer, but your safety isn't the only issue. What about the bear? Photos of grizzlies are commonplace, but the great bear is rather scarce in the Lower 48 states. What justification is there for edging closer and closer and possibly causing the bear to leave?

Some people in this situation don't think they drove the bear away because it nonchalantly walks off rather than galloping away in terror. Typical bear behavior. If two bears were in a similar situation, the subordinate animal would simply amble off long before the other bear got close. If a bear that's aware of you moves off in the other direction, you can be almost certain it's reacting to you. Whether it runs away or slowly waddles into the forest, you're probably the reason it's leaving.

For most aspiring bear photographers, taking pictures of a trained bear or visiting a bear-viewing area managed by a state or federal agency is the only way to go. No matter where you go afield in search of bear photographs, follow these guidelines:

1. Check on local regulations governing the proper distance to maintain between yourself and bears. Different places have different rules, and in parks like Katmai there's one set of guidelines for habituated bears at Brooks Camp and another set of rules for the rest of the park. Designated bear-viewing areas with habituated bears generally have their own rules and guidelines and visitors must know what they are.

2. Never feed bears, and do not try to attract bears with food or garbage.

3. If you find yourself close to a bear and you see behavior that tells you the bear is nervous (see the chapter "Bear Evolution, Biology, and Behavior"), back off at an appropriate moment and give the bear all the space it wants.

4. If you're photographing grizzlies at a location with trees, try to set up near a climbable tree. Remember, you want to climb the tree when it seems like a dangerous situation might be developing. It's impossible to climb to a safe height after a bear has begun a charge.

5. If the bear moves away, don't follow it.

6. Never approach bears.

> Everybody who is knowledgeable about bears has long had concerns about Timothy Treadwell and the message he was giving to the public.
>
> —*Sterling Miller,* Death in the Grizzly Maze

In the fall of 2003, Timothy Treadwell, co-author of *Among Grizzlies,* star of Discovery Channel's *Grizzly Diaries,* a well-known grizzly bear aficionado featured on *Late Night with David Letterman, The Rosie O'Donnell Show,* and NBC's *Dateline,* was killed and eaten by a bear in Katmai National Park. Treadwell had spent the past thirteen summers on the coast of Katmai living among one of the densest concentrations of brown bears on the continent. He gained a reputation as a "bear whisperer" who had "relationships" with bears. He gave them cute names like Mr. Chocolate, Mrs. Goodbear, and Boodles. They were his "friends." On camera, he'd chat with nearby bears, sing to them, and maniacally tell them "I love you, I love you, I love you." Above all, Treadwell was famous for getting close to wild grizzlies—dangerously close. He even touched them.

Treadwell didn't send one wrong message—he sent many wrong messages, and some of them are dangerous. Here are four important points about Timothy Treadwell, his relationship with bears, and the messages he delivered.

1. THE SECRETS TO TREADWELL'S SUCCESS. Since Treadwell was able to get up close and personal with bears in Katmai, Alaska, is it all right for you to try the same thing in Yellowstone, Banff, or other places? No. Absolutely not. Eric Wenum, a biologist who handles bear–human conflicts for the Montana Department of Fish, Wildlife, and Parks, says, "To walk out and try to touch a bear here, oh man, it's not going to go so well."[3]

For one thing, bears on the coast of Katmai require less personal space than a typical grizzly—and once you do encroach on a Katmai bear's personal space, it's not as likely to charge as a typical grizzly. This is because Katmai's bears are often well fed on salmon and other food. They're fairly well socialized from feeding in close proximity with each other, especially at salmon streams. In the words of biologist Tom Smith, "high densities of food generate high densities of bears, which, in order to access these rich forage resources, adjust their intraspecific tolerance to accommodate cospecifics at very

Don't imitate Timothy Treadwell's behavior around bears. (photo: Timothy Treadwell)

close quarters without aggressive (read "injurious") interactions."[4]

Is it safe to say Katmai's grizzlies are less aggressive than other bears? "Not at all," says Tom Smith. "They can just as easily dismantle a human as can any interior bear. It's just that one has to get so much closer to trigger that response. So it boils down to a phenomenon (high social tolerance) that is bear–bear mediated and subsequently generalized to humans."[5]

To use ballpark figures, I'd say you encroach on the personal space of a Katmai coastal bear at a distance of 40 yards. The distance for a typical bear elsewhere is around 100 yards. Once you encroach on the bear's personal space, a Katmai bear will move away 99 times out of 100, while a typical grizzly will charge 10 times out of 100. During surprise encounters at close range, a typical grizzly is far more likely to charge than a coastal brown bear. I want to emphasize again that this is a generalization; behavior varies from generalizations; they vary from bear to bear and situation to situation, which brings us to our next point.

Treadwell was familiar with the individual behavioral characteristics of many bears at two locations in Katmai. It takes months of direct observation to really learn the behavioral characteristics of a

(continued on next page)

(continued from previous page)

specific bear. You can't do it in a few minutes or a couple of hours. You're unlikely to know the first thing about the behavior of a bear you encounter in Yellowstone or Banff. Since you can't predict if a bear will go into fight or flight mode at a distance of 62 yards or 162 yards, it's risky to approach an unfamiliar bear. Worse, if the bear does charge, you won't know if it's going to pull up a few feet away or make contact.

Furthermore, bears at one of Treadwell's hangouts, Hallo Bay, were accustomed to being in close quarters with people—and not just Treadwell. He portrayed himself as a lone man in the vast Alaska wilderness, but several local bear-viewing outfits brought in clients on a daily basis. In an article about bear viewing on the coast of Katmai, specifically Hallo Bay, Tom Smith said "I've seen 60 people there at one time, and it's not a big place."[6] The Hallo Bay bears learned to tolerate people at relatively close range. To a degree, they were habituated to humans. Grizzly bears in the backcountry of Yellowstone, Banff, or almost anywhere else are not habituated to people. Not at all. Approaching an unfamiliar bear is a suicidal gamble.

2. BIOLOGISTS VS. THE BEAR WHISPERER. Biologists at designated bear viewing areas like Alaska's McNeil River and Pack Creek learn to distinguish individual bears. Treadwell did the same at his hangouts in Katmai. Treadwell and the biologists discovered the tolerance level of individual bears. When you get within 42 yards of Mrs. Goodbear, she gets uncomfortable and moves away. You can get within 16 yards of Igor the Terrible before he gets uncomfortable, but then he's going to make a short rush at you. Only Treadwell billed himself as a bear whisperer for learning about these tolerance levels. Only Treadwell claimed the bears were his "friends." Only Treadwell claimed he had "relationships" with bears. "If you come out here and do what I do, you will die," said Treadwell in Werner Herzog's film *Grizzly Man*. "But I do it right. I love these animals enough, I respect them enough, that they allow me to do this."

The bears didn't allow Treadwell to get close because they were his friends; they allowed Treadwell—and a host of other people—to get close simply because bears can be fairly tolerant under the right conditions. In contrast to most bear-viewing guides who behave ethically and back off when they see that they're stressing a bear,

Treadwell pushed the tolerance of bears to the absolute limit. On his videos, you see nervous bears salivating. You see thoroughly agitated bears rocking from side to side. "Take a close look at the videos of him getting close to bears," notes BYU professor Tom Smith, and "it becomes obvious that he was doing little more than harassing them...they just put up with him because they didn't know what else to do with this human being who kept getting in their faces."

3. DO AS I SAY, NOT AS I DO. Timothy Treadwell's website, *www.grizzlypeople.com,* warns readers to never approach within 100 yards of a grizzly, a rule Treadwell obviously ignored. Much has been made of Treadwell's efforts to educate people about bears, especially his ability to get kids excited about them. According to Treadwell's website, he reached 10,000 school kids a year. As any elementary school teacher will tell you, "do as I say, not as I do," does not work with kids. When kids see photos and film with Treadwell only a few feet away from bears, they aren't going to pay any attention to what he said—stay 100 yards away. They're going do what he did—get dangerously close to bears.

4. BEARS ARE NOT CLAIRVOYANT. Livingston, Montana photographer Tom Murphy, who leads groups of photographers on tours of Yellowstone, says, "Some people have this new-age thinking that bears can read your mind, that you're benign." This idea probably took hold back in the 1960s, after hunter/naturalist Andy Russell published *Grizzly Country.* "I am convinced that animals have extrasensory perception... there were times when a certain subtle communication seemed to exist wherein we were granted certain liberties and a measure of trust far beyond ordinary human-wild animal relationship."[7]

Treadwell and an alarming number of photographers convinced themselves that bears intuitively know whether a person's intentions are good or bad. According to this logic, bears can distinguish between a hunter who wants a freezer full of bear meat and a friendly photographer. This is a mighty convenient belief, because if anything goes wrong, the bear is at fault, not the photographer. After all, the bear should have known the photographer meant no harm. To a certain degree, bears read and respond to human body language. That's as far as it goes. Bears can't read our minds. Bears do not have ESP. Bears are not clairvoyant.

FISHING

Sometimes when I wade out in a stream while I'm fishing in Alaska, I remember photos that show a fisherman in a similar situation, except there's a bear on the bank behind him and he's obviously not aware of the bear. Watch that backcast. Glance up and down the stream periodically. Fishing in bear country can be a more thrilling pastime than you bargained for.

Black bears, brown bears, and humans all like fish, and this can bring us in close proximity to each other on noisy rivers and brush-choked streams. The noise and limited visibility make it difficult to detect one another. If you fish in bear country, you need to be bear conscious while walking to fishing sites, when actually fishing, and when camping, cooking, and storing food.

If you keep the fish you catch for a meal, gut and clean them away from camping areas. Don't bring them back to camp for cleaning, and don't clean them on the shoreline near someone else's camp. Avoid getting fish odors on your gear and clothes. Puncture the fish's air bladder

When fishing in bear country, glance up and down the stream periodically.

so it doesn't float, and throw the viscera into swift or deep water far enough out in a stream or lake so that it doesn't wash ashore. When you're done cooking your fish, properly dispose of any fish remains (cooked or otherwise) in the water.

Curious bears might check out any canoe or kayak they find on a shoreline; if that canoe or kayak smells or tastes like fish, you could find yourself patching your boat. Because fish have such a strong odor, you need to be fastidious about cleaning yourself and your gear after handling fish.

MOUNTAIN BIKING

> Off-road mountain biking in the grizzly country of the contiguous United States should be avoided. Habitat fragmentation and other serious threats are enough harassment. Besides, we have plenty of trails to ride outside of bear country.
>
> Drew Ross, *Bears* magazine, 1996

> I have a real problem with mountain bikes, or jet-powered pogo sticks or any other mechanical contrivance in the wilderness. I absolutely reject the idea that you can have a wilderness experience on a bike.
>
> Harvey Manning, *Backpacker* magazine, 1996

When grizzlies were classified as a threatened species in the Lower 48 states under the Endangered Species Act in 1975, hunters, horsemen, and other "traditional" users of grizzly country outnumbered backpackers by a wide margin. Imagine the outcry if the hunters and horsemen had said "backpacking in the grizzly country of the contiguous United States should be avoided. Habitat fragmentation and other serious threats are enough harassment. Besides, you have plenty of trails to hike on outside of bear country."

Maybe it's not a good idea to make land management policies based on the argument that "we were here first." But in a 1996 article titled "Some Basic Truths of Mountain Biking," the *San Francisco Examiner's* Tom Stienstra inadvertently hit on several persuasive arguments for not riding mountain bikes in grizzly bear country. Stienstra, a newcomer to the sport of mountain biking, mentioned, "It's quiet. Bikes are perfect for riding obscure dirt roads in national forests. Since bikes are quiet and fast, you can see a lot of wildlife, especially deer, because you are upon them before they have a chance to react."[8]

When you come upon grizzly bears before they have a chance to react, you have violated one of the cardinal rules of safe travel in grizzly country and placed yourself in a dangerous situation. "The increase in mountain biking and the temper of a surprised grizzly," noted *Bears* magazine, "sounds as volatile a mix as gasoline and fire."

Indeed, Jasper National Park had fifteen biker–bear incidents between 1987 and 1995, including one man who was clawed and bitten. There have also been incidents and injuries in Banff, Kluane, and Denali National Parks.

Part of the problem is a "fun-hog" attitude that many mountain bikers share; they treat the natural world as an outdoor playground. Consider the Jackson, Wyoming, mountain biker who was injured by a grizzly in September of 2004 near Togwotee Pass.[9] Standard etiquette in grizzly country is to make noise to avoid surprising a bear, especially in prime bear habitat. The mountain biker wasn't making any noise. Conventional wisdom is to travel a group of two or more. The mountain biker got separated from a companion and was traveling solo. But here's the big thing. Whitebark pine seeds are one of the four most important foods for bears in the Yellowstone region. They're the most important natural food during the fall when bears go into a feeding frenzy (*hyperphagia*) to put on weight for hibernation. There aren't that many stands of whitebark pine in the Yellowstone region. Yet the mountain biker was "right in the middle of a whitebark pine forest" when he had his unpleasant encounter with a grizzly. Why not ride somewhere else, if only for your own safety? Why bother the grizzly bears in such an important place at such an important time?

To avoid unpleasant encounters, a brochure by the Interagency Grizzly Bear Committee and Wyoming Department of Fish and Game gives people three standard warnings. First, check on local regulations to make sure mountain bikes are allowed on the trail or road you plan to use. Second, travel in a group. Last, "Don't surprise bears—be especially cautious when traveling fast downhill on a trail with blind curves. Slow down and make noise before rounding such bends."[10]

Some people put bear bells on their handlebars or saddle so they constantly clang along bumpy roads and trails. As I discuss in the chapter "Camping and Travel Tips," making noise raises ethical and esthetic considerations. You drive away bears and other wildlife, and you drive other people nuts. Harvey Manning, author of numerous hiking guides, recently said, "[I]t's impossible to be nice when I'm driven off a trail by a pack of yipping, chattering youth dressed in their sister's underwear."[11] His comment infuriated mountain bikers in Washington State, but I believe Manning expressed how bears feel about having mountain bikers zoom through their backyard.

Cross-country skiers should watch out for bears.

CROSS-COUNTRY SKIING

Cross-country skiers, especially skiers camping and cooking on overnight trips, need to be aware that bears might be out and about. On March 8, 2001, a Grand Teton National Park employee cross-country skiing in Upper Berry Creek was injured by a grizzly bear. A National Park Service news release about the incident noted that "Bears can become active during late February and early March, especially during mild winters."[12]

Some bears den late. For instance, in Yellowstone Park, a grizzly bear was spotted running down the road at Mud Volcano on December 6.[13] Denning bears sometimes take brief winter walkabouts. For example, on January 5, 2006, U.S. Forest Service backcountry ranger Craig Lang saw a grizzly near the Sun River in Montana's Bob Marshall Wilderness. Montana Department of Fish, Wildlife and Parks wildlife biologist Gary Olson explained, "Bears will on occasion come out of their winter den, wander around, and go back in."[14]

Black bears usually shimmy down trees rear-end first, but young bears don't always play by the rules.

Close Encounters

STAND YOUR GROUND

Here's the best all-around rule for handling close encounters with bears: If a bear that's aware of you approaches you, stand your ground. That sounds macho, but I've "frozen in fear" and it's as effective as puffing your chest out and daring a bear to take one step closer.

Whether you're facing a charging grizzly or a bold black bear entering your campsite, stand your ground. In certain situations with certain types of bears, you can do more than just stand your ground, but standing your ground won't make a bad situation worse. Running probably will. Running is likely to elicit a chase response. Trying to climb a tree will probably elicit a chase, too. Biologist Tom Beck advises that tree climbing to escape a black bear is a mistake. "In antagonistic encounters between black bears, the submissive bear will often climb a tree. In most cases the dominant bear will follow, attempting to grab the fleeing bear by the hind foot and tug it down. Sound familiar? Human goes up a tree, bear responds as if human is a mangy bear, climbs tree, grabs foot, pulls him down."[1]

In *Grizzlies in the Mist*, ecologist Chuck Neal encountered a grizzly bear family 40 yards away and the sow charged: "No one can experience such a charge at this range without recognizing the folly of attempting to run or even to climb a tree. Even if a tree had been at my back I don't believe I could have reached safety in the upper branches before the bear dragged me down."[2]

According to some bear literature, bears will posture during a close encounter and turn broadside to show you how big they are. Larry Aumiller writes, "Broadside orientation of one bear as a signal to another is a widely held 'truth' that, based on my personal experience, is probably untrue. Frontal orientation is the most aggressive and dominating body position."[3]

During a close encounter with a bear, you can forget about subtle body language and focus on one point: Is the bear advancing toward you? When you have a close encounter with a bear, remember that the bear might be a little nervous, too. Huffing and a bit of foam around the bear's lips are signs of stress, not signals from the bear warning that it's about to attack. Don't assume the bear wants to kill you. A curious bear is just interested in checking you out, and even a female with cubs only wants to protect her youngsters. She might decide to threaten you or render you harmless, but she's most likely to protect her cubs by simply moving away from you.

HOW TO RECOGNIZE A PREDATORY BLACK BEAR

You're looking for a combination of body language and behavior—what Terry DeBruyn calls the bear's gestalt.

- Silence. Predatory black bears will make a silent approach on all fours. If you're engaged with a nearby bear and it's huffing, jaw-popping, clacking its teeth, or making other noises, you're hearing sounds of nervousness or distress.
- The bear will be intensely focused on you.
- The bear will approach you. Sometimes it will make a confident, open approach. Other times it will persistently make its way closer to you. As it approaches, you won't see signs of stress.
- Head up.
- Ears erect or forward. Ears forward is the position of an aggressor. Head down, neck stretched out, ears laid back is not a predatory bear, it's a bear that's nervous or feels threatened.

Slowly backing away from an approaching bear during the first few moments of an encounter is usually a bad move that will encourage a curious or predatory bear to keep pressing forward. Stand your ground. "Standing confidently means something to a bear, just as backing away shows fear," BYU professor Tom Smith told the *Fairbanks News-Miner.* "When standing your ground, your posture says to the bear, 'I'm neither submissive nor will I be easily taken down. This will cost you if you try anything with me,' whereas those who cower and back up are saying, 'Bear, you are dominant and in control of this show.'"[4]

In essence, once a bear that's 40 yards away charges you and then stops 15 yards away, you're involved in an intricate dance—the problem is that neither of you knows exactly how to lead or follow. You're both dancing impaired. When you reach a point where each of you has a choice of three moves to make, you both might step in the wrong direction and bump into each other or stomp your partner's toes.

The complexity of bear encounters makes me leery of assertions about what a bear is telling you with its body language when it turns

FACT OR FALLACY ?

FALLACY
Never make eye contact with a bear because bears perceive this as a threat.[5]

FACT
When thirty-two bear experts met in March of 2000 for the Alaska Interagency Bear Safety Education Committee, behavioral expert Terry DeBruyn said, "Making eye contact with a bear will not provoke it." The Committee said, "Eye contact will not make a situation worse." In a discussion about bear safety classes for the public, the Committee concluded that you "should keep an eye on the animal so you can see it …. A continued steady gaze is acceptable behavior… keep the bear in sight at all times so you can detect important visual clues to the bear's behavior."[6]

It's often said you should never stare at a bear during a close encounter, but after twenty-one years of watching bear–bear interactions at McNeil River, Larry Aumiller says, "[B]ears will look intently at you for a variety of reasons, but I've never felt that it was more than gaining visual information. Some bears who receive this visual inspection from another bear will become uneasy and move away. I've never felt the actual act of looking or staring at a bear conveyed any message except in the subtlest of interactions."[7]

broadside or stares intently at you or clacks its teeth. Bear encounters are not that simplistic. Biologist Polly Hessing cautions, "[B]ears may give and respond to subtle postural clues; we might miss or misinterpret these clues. I don't think that bears posture to show their size as a threat to us—I think it's part of trying to diminish the stress engendered by the situation."[8]

In *Walking with Bears,* biologist Terry DeBruyn describes a close encounter with a wild black bear he'd been trailing for years: "Nettie looks directly at me across the few feet separating us. I remain seated and look directly back, not believing as some do that bears interpret direct eye contact as an act of provocation."[9]

Both Benjamin Kilham and Ph.D biologist Stephen Stringham raised orphaned black bear cubs which sometimes brought them in close contact with mature black bears in the wild. Kilham once found himself 12 feet away from a male black bear interested in a female named Squirty, who was at Kilham's feet. Kilham was filming the action. In *Among the Bears,* Kilham wrote that if he took his eyes and the camera off the male, "he would immediately rush me .... As I had long ago learned with lesser bears, my eyes were my best defense."[10]

Stringham wrote in *Beauty Within the Beast,* that when he had close encounters with male bears in the woods, "Walking toward the animal, with my eyes locked onto him, usually sufficed to drive him away."[11]

Could staring at a nearby bear make a bad situation worse? At first glance, that appears to be what happened to Justin Kumagai in a story recounted in *Bear Attacks: The Deadly Truth.* Kumagai was making noise while digging soil samples as part of a timber sale in British Columbia. He looked up and saw a grizzly 40 yards away. The bear was staring at him. They locked eyes for a second and the bear charged. According to *Deadly Truth* author James Gary Shelton, when Kumagai "made eye contact with the bear, it triggered the attack."[12]

It did? Maybe the bear charged because Kumagai was wearing a blue shirt. Perhaps the bear charged because Kumagai was wearing citronella-based insect repellent. In all likelihood, it just took the bear a second to sense there was a person nearby, and when it grasped the situation, the bear charged. Eye contact had nothing to do with it. Kumagai could have been looking the other way and the bear still would have charged.

During a sudden encounter with a nearby bear, the odds are you won't be able to stop yourself from staring at the bear. I don't think that's going to trigger a charge. During a stand-off, or if a bear is slowly advancing toward you, it's important for you to watch the bear's behavior. If anything, watching the bear and maintaining eye contact will probably help deter the bear.

PREDATORY BLACK BEARS: THE MAKING OF A MYTH

In 1985, Stephen Herrero's *Bear Attacks* noted that a "feature of major injuries inflicted by black bears was that predation appeared to be the motive for eighteen of the twenty black bear-inflicted deaths."[13]

In contrast, grizzly bears had only preyed on a handful of people. The disparity didn't draw any comments from biologists or bear experts because it made perfect sense—there were far more black bears than grizzly bears in North America. But in 1998, British Columbia woodsman James Gary Shelton wrote, in his self-published *Bear Attacks: The Deadly Truth,* "Statistics indicate that black bears are more predacious towards humans than are grizzlies."[14] Shelton did not include any statistics to verify his claim. The book did not include citations to substantiate Shelton's remark. But Shelton kept talking about predatory black bears. In 2000, he told the *Cleveland Plain Dealer,* "There's going to be a slow, steady increase of predatory black bear attacks that will catch bear managers off guard."[15]

Next Shelton published *Bear Attacks II,* where he made the following remark about predatory black bears: "In a predatory attack, the bear is trying to kill the person for food. It takes significant resistance to survive this type of attack, and unknown to most people, black bears have a higher level of this type of aggression towards humans than do grizzly bears."[16]

In 2001, Shelton, who was described by the *Medford Mail Tribune* as "a British Columbia researcher who has written three books on bear behavior," said black bears are "five times more likely than a grizzly bear" to prey on a person. Then he added the clincher: "I'd suspect, at any time now, we'll have a predatory attack by a black bear in California or Oregon. Definitely."[17]

The more the media hyped predatory black bears, the more people began to see any casual meeting with a black bear as a potentially deadly predatory encounter. The *Anchorage Daily News* published an article titled "Hungry-Looking Black Bear Gives Hiker a Scare" in 2002. It began by saying "Gene Trumbo didn't like the look in the eyes of the big black bear. The bear, he said, looked like it was wondering what a man tasted like."[18]

While discussing bears that prey on humans with *Canadian Geographic* in 2002, Shelton again preached that "this behavior is more common with black bears" than grizzlies.[19]

(continued on next page)

(continued from previous page)

As word about predatory black bears got out, people became fearful. "McHugh Creek hiker tells of being stalked by 3 bears," said a headline in June 1, 2003 *Anchorage Daily News*. A family of black bears followed Jim Leslie, which is uncommon—but not unheard of—behavior. Any curious bear might follow a person, especially if it's habituated or food-conditioned. "I thought I was going to be dinner," said Leslie.

In 2004, yet another bear attack book was published; in *Bear Attacks: Who Survived and Why,* author Mike Lapinski stated, "For some reason as yet unknown, black bears tend to be more predatory than grizzlies toward humans."[20]

Clearly, the notion that black bears are more predatory than grizzlies toward people has taken hold. But is it true?

No. Stephen Herrero and Andrew Higgins looked at the issue when they published a scientific paper on bear attacks in *Ursus,* the quarterly journal of the IBA. Herrero and Higgins analyzed "Human Injuries Inflicted by Black Bears in British Columbia: 1960–97." There were "eighteen potentially predatory black bear attacks" out of a population of 120,000 to 160,000 black bears. There were four potentially predatory grizzly attacks out of a population of 10,000 to 13,000 grizzly bears. "We cannot conclude that predation is more likely in black bears because B.C. has approximately twelve times as many black bears as grizzly bears."[21]

BYU professor Tom Smith keeps a database on Alaska bear attacks dating back to 1900, and when he compared black bear predation on humans to grizzly bear predation on humans, he reached a similar conclusion to Herrero and Higgins. In July 2005, Smith told the *Anchorage Daily News,* "If we factor in that there are at least three times more black bears in Alaska than brown/grizzlies, we see that brown/grizzlies have actually had more than double the predacious events per 1,000 bears than black bears."[22]

In September of 2005, *Alaska* magazine published an article titled "The Bear that Never Was," by Tom Smith and biologists Steve Alstrup and Steve Herrero. They said, "There are 18 known cases in which black bears preyed upon, or attempted to prey upon, people. This behavior, combined with the greater reluctance of surprised black bears to attack people, may have resulted in skewed interpretations of the data available on black bear attacks."[23]

Clearly, a statistical fallacy combined with a healthy dose of fear mongering has created unwarranted paranoia about predatory black bears. If you find yourself in close quarters with a black bear, I can guarantee you won't be able to recognize a predatory bear by "the look in its eyes." On page 116, I explain key behavioral differences between a predatory black bear, and a black bear that's merely curious, food-conditioned, or frightened.

If A Bear Attacks

If a bear attacks you—physically touches you—then you have two alternatives: Fight back or play dead. Your response depends on the situation.

If a black bear or grizzly bear enters your tent at night, assume the bear is in a predatory mode and fight back by any means available. People have killed bears with little pocket knives and bonked them on the head with rocks. Hit the bear with your boots. Punch it in the nose. Fight back as if your life depends on it—because it probably does. Some people keep pepper spray in their tent just for this particular occasion. You'd better hope it deters the bear for a while, because you will be incapacitated after spraying inside your tent.

Even if a bear pulls your companion out of a tent, it's not too late to save him or her. Steve French, in his paper on bear attacks (which was written for medical professionals and might make you a little queasy), notes, "Predatory grizzly and black bears rarely kill their victims before consuming them. After dragging them away from camp usually less than a few hundred feet, they concentrate their efforts towards soft tissue or visceral consumption and the victims frequently remain alive for an hour or more. Therefore, a quick, aggressive, and unified response by companions can potentially save the victim's life. Approaching a predatory bear in the dark while it is trying to feed on a human victim is certainly not without risk but is probably the victim's only chance for survival. This action has been successful on several occasions."[24]

In places like Yosemite and the Boundary Waters Canoe Area, it's common for food-habituated black bears to enter campsites. You want to dominate curious or food-conditioned bears. When one walks into your backcountry campsite, bang pots and pans. Clap your hands. Shout at it. Throw things toward it. The closer the bear gets, the more you need to increase the level of your response. The more people the better, although you should be careful not to surround a bear.

FACT OR FALLACY ?

FALLACY
Bears will warn you before attacking.

FACT
Bears attack without warning. During a sudden encounter with a bear, there's no time for the bear to express its fear, anxiety, or anger. Boom—it just charges. Predatory bears hunting humans, elk calves, and other prey don't jaw-pop, huff, roar, or make a commotion—and why would they? A bear stalking an elk calf or a human is in stealth mode; if the bear made a commotion, it would scare away its prey. Jaw popping and huffing are behaviors of a stressed bear, not a bear in a predatory mode. As biologist Stephen Stringham states in *Beauty Within the Beast*, "Predators don't threaten prey, which are easiest to ambush while calm and oblivious to the predator's intention, so they can be approached closely before the fatal charge and attack."[25]

Yosemite Park bear literature used to advise people to throw "rocks at" black bears entering camp until a troop of Boy Scouts stoned a bear to death in 1996. (One of the leaders brained the bear with a fist-sized rock.) Now the Park Service tells people to throw small rocks in the bear's direction, but not directly at the bear.[26] Use something the size of a golf ball or smaller.

The further a bear gets into your camp, the more difficult it will be to drive it out. The sooner you take aggressive actions, the better the chances of forcing the bear to leave. If the bear is already into your food when you first see it, leave it alone. If it gets into your food despite the commotion you make, leave it alone. The only exception to this rule might be in a remote area where the loss of your food could mean weeks of hunger. If you bother a bear that has your food, you might end up with a few bites and scratches. In almost all circumstances, the best thing to do is leave the bear alone and come back after the bear is gone to clean up.

Behaviorally, it can be difficult to distinguish a predatory bear from one that is simply curious or food-conditioned. One difference with black bears is that a food-conditioned bear may make threat displays to get you out of the way. Predatory bears don't threaten or vocalize. There's no huffing or blowing, no rushing two steps toward you and slapping the ground. A threatened bear will have its ears pinned back; a predatory bear will have its ears cocked forward and make a silent approach. Predatory bears are intensely interested in their victim. They may try to circle behind you, but they keep pressing and bearing in. If a black bear seems to be stalking you, keep an eye on it and don't let it circle behind you. Always face the animal. Keep your eyes on it. The same aggressive actions that usually drive away a curious or food-conditioned bear entering your camp are likely to rout a predatory bear, too.

Be wary of a bear that's aware of you and approaching on all fours.

Bluff Charges

Grizzlies often bluff-charge a potential threat, sometimes stopping just a few feet away. But it's impossible to tell when a charge is a bluff, when the bear intends to cuss somebody out, and when the bear means business.

—Scott McMillion, *Mark of the Grizzly*[27]

Do bears really make bluff charges? This implies that a bear spots a forester picking berries and consciously decides—before charging—to race within 12 feet of the forester and then stop. "Ha, ha. I was just bluffing."

Is this actually what happens? In *Walking with Bears,* biologist Terry DeBruyn has this to say about charging bears: "I have heard these displays termed bluff charges, and while that may be an apt description of their outcome, I'm uncertain that bluffing is in the bear's mind at the outset. It's quite possible that such charges are intended to provoke a response, the outcome depending on that response—stand pat, it's a bluff;

A bear's remarkable sense of smell will lead it to your food cache or any interesting odor—inluding propane canisters.

waver and run, it's a rout."[28] Furthermore, AIBSEC guidelines say that bear safety literature should not include the phrase "bluff-charge."

DON'T RUN—DON'T RETREAT—DON'T CLIMB TREES

When you startle a grizzly at close range and it charges, I don't believe the bear is bluffing. These charges are real and, to some degree, your actions determine the outcome of the encounter. Even when a curious sub-adult grizzly makes a half-hearted hop-charge toward you, if you take a couple of quick steps back or break and run, your action changes the dynamics of the encounter and the bear may keep coming at you. People who run are far more likely to get knocked down than people who stand their ground.

Tree-climbing after a grizzly bear charges you is likely to make a bad situation worse. Bears usually get to the tree before people are out of reach and drag them out of the tree by the foot. Two people have been killed in such a fall. In each case, after the person hit the ground, the bear left the scene.

You need to make good decisions when you have a surprise encounter with a bear. Once you realize there's a bear nearby that seems to be aware of you, make sure it has positively identified you as a human. It might not have a clear take on what you are—so never try to hide. Hiding could draw the bear closer to identify you. Don't yell loudly but do talk to the bear so it hears a human voice. Don't make any quick movements. Slowly, very slowly, step away from trees, rocks, or brush that block the bear's view of you. Help the bear see you. You want it to know you're human.

If it charges, stand your ground. It might swerve at the last second and run by you. If a charging bear stops a few feet short of you and you're having a stand-off, keep still at first. Any quick movement could trigger an attack. Don't shout. Talk quietly to the bear. Give the bear a moment to gather its wits. There's a good chance it will leave. If it doesn't, then when the bear is stationary, you can try to s-l-o-w-l-y quarter away at an oblique angle. Keep your eyes on the bear. You need to see how it responds to your movement. If movement agitates the bear, stop moving.

PLAYING DEAD

Don't even think about playing dead when a bear is still 10 or 20 yards away. There have been numerous instances where people flopped down and played dead too soon; the bear then came over to investigate.

FACT OR FALLACY ?

FALLACY

Play dead for a grizzly; fight back against a black bear. The rule of thumb in bear country used to be: Play dead for a grizzly, fight back against a black bear. The thought was that most grizzly bear attacks are defensive in nature. You startle a nearby grizzly, and it perceives you as a threat and charges. If you play dead, you're no longer a threat, and the bear goes away. Conversely, most serious black bear attacks are predatory, so you fight back. Play dead and you're lunch. This rule of thumb seemed simple enough, but people got things mixed up and played dead at the wrong time. They played dead when they were obviously being stalked by predatory black bears during the day. They played dead when black bears came into their tents at night. They played dead when approached by curious grizzly bears.

FACT

Play dead if a defensive bear makes contact; fight back against a predatory bear. It doesn't matter if you're facing a black bear or a grizzly bear, your response should be based on the bear's behavior.

Sometimes the bears just batted the people around, other times the bear began eating them.

When facing a charging bear, don't play dead when you think contact is imminent—wait for the bear to make contact. Tom Smith says, "I tell my field personnel to never lay down for a bear—never."

Smith points out that "by prematurely laying down one says to the bear, 'I'm subordinate, passive… yours.' As long as we remain standing we remain a viable threat. Bears test things and they may test us by lunging, circling, or moving close. By not folding your hand, so to speak, you are saying, 'I am not passive or subordinate. If you engage with me you will pay."[29]

While startled grizzlies are the bears most likely to charge people, there have been a few cases where people surprised a female black bear with cubs at close range and she charged and attacked. If a female black bear with cubs attacks, this is one occasion when you should play dead. You can assume that she's protecting her cubs rather than launching a predatory attack. If the attack persists more than a minute or so, it's time to fight back. Never play dead with an attacking black bear unless you are certain you have startled a female with cubs. In any other situation, fight back immediately.

In places like Glacier or Waterton Park, a bear could come bursting out of the brush and attack you before you have any idea of whether it is a black bear or a grizzly, a solitary bear or a female with cubs. Because it's rare for black bears to charge and attack people, I'd assume I had startled a grizzly and play dead. If you play dead, a startled grizzly generally does not cause serious injuries.

Neither does a female black bear with cubs that has been surprised. Fighting back is likely to increase the severity of your injuries. However, if a bear works you over for more than a minute or so, reconsider the situation. When an attack lasts too long and it seems the bear has lost its initial fury and settled down to eat, playing dead isn't going to save your life. You have to fight back.

When a bear fights or wrestles, it directs most bites and blows to its opponent's head, so you want to protect your head if you're attacked. It's best to lie face-down on the ground with your legs slightly spread apart, interlock your hands behind your head, and tuck your elbows tight against the side of your head. You'll have a low center of gravity and a bear will have to flip you over to get at your face and head. A second technique, one you might instinctively use, is to curl up in a ball with your hands behind your head and your legs curled up beneath your chest. The problem with this technique is that balls roll.

Don't get up right away when the bear leaves. Sometimes bears wait and watch; any movement could trigger another attack. As Steve French dryly notes in his paper on bear attacks, "[v]ictims who are attacked from a close encounter situation and who immediately protect themselves and do not try to resist typically receive outpatient injuries. However, those who try to get up and leave after the initial attack but before the bear leaves the area typically receive much more severe injuries during a second attack, requiring multiple surgical procedures resulting in permanent cosmetic and/or functional disabilities."

French also notes that if you try to fend off a bear with your hand, forearm, or arm, "bears can readily cause significant neurovascular injuries to these structures."

If you're with a group of people and a bear charges, the most active person in the group is the one most likely to get nailed.[30]

DANCING WITH BEARS

Dance #1

You're hiking in British Columbia when you hear branches snapping, you look up, and you see a grizzly just 35 yards away in full charge. It takes your mind a moment to process what's happening. There's no time to use a firearm or pepper spray.

- Stand your ground.
- Don't run. Don't back away slowly. Don't shout and wave your arms. Don't move.
- Don't play dead until contact is made.

Dance #2

A charging grizzly or black bear suddenly stops 4 yards away.

- Watch the bear. Face the bear.
- Don't shout, but do talk quietly to the bear.
- Give the bear a few moments to move off.
- No quick moves. If you have pepper spray in hand, use it. If you have to reach for your pepper spray, move in slow motion and be as quiet as possible.
- When the bear is not moving, you can try backing away, one slow step at a time. If this appears to agitate the bear, stand still.

Dance #3

A non-defensive bear approaches. This is not a bear charging in self-defense after a sudden, close up encounter. It's just a bear you bumped into on a trail. It's aware of you, and now it's walking in your direction. You don't know if it's a curious black bear, a young grizzly bear asserting its dominance, a food-conditioned black bear looking for a snack, or a predatory grizzly.

- Stand your ground.
- Face the bear and keep your eyes on the bear.
- Get your pepper spray or firearm ready. Quickly assess the situation: Are you blocking the bear's travel corridor or standing between the bear and a food source?
- Talk calmly to the bear.
- Move out of the bear's travel path. Go back at an oblique (45 degree) angle. That might be all the bear wants. If possible, go to the uphill side of the trail so you look bigger.

If the bear alters its travel route to follow you and its attention is directed at you:

- Stop. Stand your ground.
- Be the aggressor. Shout. Stare at the bear. Slap your hiking stick into a tree trunk.
- Stamp your feet and take a quick step toward the bear.
- If it keeps coming, use your spray or firearm.

Years of experience in Denali and other national parks have proven that properly secured bear resistant food containers work. (photo: Richard Garcia)

Guns and Pepper Spray

GUNS

When people take firearms afield, it's usually because they're afraid of grizzlies. Before you take your trusty 30-30 off the fireplace mantle and strike off for grizzly country, here are a few points to consider. You're not likely to be charged by a grizzly unless you startle a bear at 60 yards or less. A grizzly can cover 60 yards in 4 to 5 seconds. It will be hurtling toward you at 30 or more miles per hour. Your target area is only about 12 square inches. For bear defense, the U.S. Fish and Wildlife Service in Alaska and the Department of Renewable Resources for Canada's Northwest Territories recommend a minimum of a 12-gauge 3-inch Magnum shotgun firing 1-ounce slugs or a 30-06 with a 200-grain bullet.[1] (The Fish and Wildlife Service does not authorize the use of buck shot for its personnel.) Professional hunting guides in Alaska usually rely on a .375 H&H Magnum shooting 300-grain bullets. A .375 H&H magnum has about half again the power of a 30-06 and makes Dirty Harry's famous .44 Magnum look like a squirt gun.

When you take all these factors into consideration, it's clear there's no sense taking a gun afield unless you're proficient with it. Very proficient. In order to "qualify" to carry a gun afield in Alaska, U.S. Forest Service employees using a .375 H&H Magnum must put nine shots (three sets of three) in a 12-inch circle at a range of 15 to 40 yards in 10 seconds or less.[2] That's a reasonable standard for beginners that can be met after a weekend of training—just remember that shooting paper targets is one thing and shooting charging grizzlies is an altogether different matter.

If you honestly expect to drop a charging bear with a firearm, your actions have to be instinctual. My friend Hod Coburn was a professional hunting guide in Alaska for years, and Hod says, "If it's the real deal with a bruin, all this is going to be done from start to stop in about five seconds, max."[3] Before you go afield with a weapon, you need to decide when you're going to shoot. You have to mentally draw a line in the sand at whatever distance you're comfortable with. Bear in mind that if you just stand your ground when a grizzly charges, it most likely will break off its charge at a distances of 5 to 25 yards. People with firearms have wounded or killed bears that would have stopped if someone had just aimed a hiking staff at the bear and said "Bang."

Most bear experts draw the line at 5 to 7 yards or less.[4] Have a set distance in mind. The instant there's a close encounter with a bear, ready your weapon and pick a rock or bush 5 to 7 yards away. Shoot when the bear reaches that point. People who don't draw a line in the sand are prone to freeze when they face a charging bear. They're mesmerized by the bear and don't shoot until the last second. Sometimes it's too late.

Although a few people have managed to kill a bear with a pistol, more animals have only been wounded by these underpowered and difficult-to-master weapons. Wounding a bear at close range can change the dynamics of an encounter from an agitated bear defending itself to an angry bear attacking you. Pistols and pepper spray have about the same effective range. Most people would have a much better chance of hitting the bear with pepper spray. Pepper spray would stop the bear just as often as a .357 or .44 Magnum, and pepper spray doesn't kill or wound bears.

Firing a warning shot probably just wastes ammo and increases the risk of your gun jamming when you quickly chamber a second round. In particular, short people with short arms have a tendency to "short-stroke" pump action shotguns. Most hunters carry bolt action rifles, and the same short-stroke problem can occur under duress. For example, in 2004 Alaska hunting guide Scott Newman was carrying a .416 Remington Magnum and following a wounded brown bear when the bear charged him. He shot once, then "worked the bolt to chamber a second round but 'short-stroked' it, jamming the rifle."[5]

Professional hunting guides don't fire warning shots because warning shots almost never change the behavior of a bear.

Carrying firearms can give you the peace of mind to stand your ground during an encounter. You might save your life without pulling the trigger. You'll have to fight against overconfidence; don't go anywhere or do anything you wouldn't consider doing if you were unarmed.

DANGEROUS MISTAKES WITH FIREARMS

"The truth is that people don't shoot particularly well under stressful situations like a bear attack."

—*Christopher Batin, "Bear Attacks,"*
Outdoor Life, *August 2003*

When *Anchorage Daily News* Outdoors Editor Craig Medred first spotted the grizzly bear family in the fall of 1992, the bruins were about 100 feet away. The bears had sensed Medred first, and they were milling around, trying to figure out what to do. Medred should have readied his weapon, a pistol chambered for the powerful .454 Casull. He didn't.[6]

When Montana hunting guide Joe Heimer and his client first spotted the grizzly family in November, 1996, the bears weren't aware of them, so the people retreated to cover about 30–35 yards away. Heimer did ready a 7mm Remington Magnum rifle.[7]

Both men should have decided—before ever going afield—that if they were charged by a bear they'd shoot when the bruin got within 5–7 yards or some other set distance. Evidently, they didn't.

The sow Medred was watching charged. "I hesitated to shoot," claims Medred, "thinking she was bluffing."[8] Not until the charging bear was 2 feet away did Medred tell himself to get the gun up. And by then it was too late. The bear knocked Medred down and injured him before he could get off a shot.

The sow Heimer was watching detected him and charged. He held fire until "her head was no more than 8 inches from the rifle's muzzle." Then he shot and missed. The bear severely injured both Heimer and his client.

If you're going to rely on firearms for protection from bears, here are four tips that will prevent you from freezing in fear or panicking and firing a wild shot at the last moment.

1. You should decide at what distance you'll shoot an approaching bear before you go afield. I recommend 5 to 7 yards. It's common for charging bears to stop short of making contact, provided you hold your ground.[9]

2. Be aware that most charges occur when you startle a bear at a distance of 60 yards or less. If you find yourself in close quarters with a bear, ready your weapon.
3. Pick out a rock, tree, or some other object 5 to 7 yards away and tell yourself to shoot when the bear reaches that point.
4. Never assume a charging bear is bluffing. Biologists and bear experts don't believe that bears make bluff charges. Even if you disagree with this assessment, consider the following exchange from *Mark of the Grizzly*. Alaskan hunter Dale Bagley startled a nearby grizzly feeding on a moose carcass. The bear charged. Bagley fired. Author Scott McMillion asked Bagley, "Could it have been a bluff charge?" Bagley responded, "At 40 feet and coming fast, I'd be foolish to assume that."[10]

PEPPER SPRAY

The spray is better than nothing, but I don't want to be in a situation where I have to use it.
—Biologist Chuck Jonkel, *Field & Stream*, 1987

Chuck Jonkel is a biologist who helped develop pepper spray during the early 1980s. Although Jonkel found that pepper spray effectively deterred both grizzly and black bears under laboratory conditions, people wondered whether it would work in real-life situations. Most of all, people wondered whether it would stop a charging grizzly bear.

Pepper spray is made from super-hot ground-up peppers (oleoresin capsicum) in a pressurized container. Cans of pepper spray usually weigh around a pound and are roughly 2 inches in diameter and 8 to 9 inches tall; they're much larger than the little keychain or purse-size canisters of mace. You can't take your pepper spray on a plane; you'll be stopped at airport security and your pepper spray will be confiscated. It's also illegal to put pepper spray in your checked baggage. Always warn bush pilots with small planes that you have pepper spray. They can attach it to the wing strut on a wheeled plane or put it in the floats of a float plane. These precautions are necessary because if a can of pepper spray goes off in a small plane, down you go.

Just as there would be trouble if a can of pepper spray went off in a plane, an accidental discharge in your vehicle could be disastrous. At the very least, carry pepper spray in a double layer of resealable plastic bags. Most pepper spray companies sell good containers.

Don't leave pepper spray on the dashboard of your vehicle where it's going to bake in the sun. For long-term storage, the optimum temperature is 50 to 70 degrees Fahrenheit. It's easier on the can's seals if the temperature is constant. Pepper spray has a shelf life of one to three years; there's usually an expiration date marked on the can.

Pepper spray is equipped with a plastic safety tab that is not child-proof. At home and in the field, you must secure pepper spray from children. Pepper spray is burning hot on the skin, and I never want to find out what it feels like to get hit in the eyes. If you get it on your skin, wash it off with soap and either cool water or milk. If possible, wash your face with a non-tearing soap or something like baby shampoo. If you get pepper spray in your eyes, flush them with copious amounts of water. People who wear contacts will no doubt remove them immediately. Due to the porosity of contact lenses, you'll probably never wear that particular pair again. Try cleaning them with an appropriate lens-cleaning solution, but they may sting when you put them back in. You should check with your optometrist.

If you're going to buy pepper spray, get at least two cans—one to test-fire, and one for later use. The $40–$50 you pay to spray a can that's empty in a few seconds might seem like a lot of money, but it would be penny-wise and pound foolish to rely on a tool you've never used before to stop a charging grizzly.

Biologist Tom Beck suggests the following test. Practice firing at a piece of cardboard or scrap plywood. Observe the pattern of the spray. It leaves a bright orange-red residue. Run a fingertip over the residue and then lick your fingertip. You'll find that the pepper spray is unbelievably hot.

If you're experienced with firearms, the first time you pick up a can of pepper spray and aim it, you're likely to point the nozzle at your face. After you figure out which way to aim it and test fire the stuff, you'll probably be surprised at the limited range. It really doesn't go far. You might also be surprised at the loud hissing noise the can makes and the brightly colored spray. Make sure you fire downwind.

I strongly recommend taking two cans afield when you're in grizzly country, particularly on overnight trips. Let's say you have to spray a bear on day two of a five-day hike in Jasper National Park. You're going to be a bear-conscious bundle of nerves for awhile. If you just used your one and only can of bear spray, you won't have any means of protection for the next three days.

Pepper spray fires out in a foggy mist like insect spray. Depending on the manufacturer, it has a maximum range of 18 to 30 feet. One manufacturer cautions that "the most effective range to stop an attack is half the maximum range." In a 10-mile-per-hour crosswind, the spray from pepper spray will start drifting sideways at a distance of about 8 feet. In a hard rain, the kind of rain that's common in Southeast Alaska and along the coast of British Columbia, pepper spray has a shorter range. Although cold weather—temperatures less than 40 degrees Fahrenheit—affects the performance of pepper spray (or any other aerosol product), you can carry it inside your jacket during the day, and put it in your sleeping bag at night.

This brings up one of the problems of relying on pepper spray too much: when you need it the most—when you startle a bear—you may not be able to get to it quick enough. That's exactly what happened to Kelly Krpata and Kim Taffer on a trail in Glacier Park in August of 2000. According to park spokeswoman Amy Vanderbilt, the pair was hiking on the Swiftcurrent Trail when "the bear came at them in a full-blown charge from about 50 yards away. He [Krpata] did have pepper spray, but he didn't have time to pull it out."[11]

Krpata had his pepper spray attached to a shoulder strap on his pack where it was quickly accessible, yet the charge happened so suddenly, he didn't have time to reach it. T.J. Langley, Jr. had a similar experience on Yellowstone Park's Black Butte trail in 1999. He stumbled into a grizzly family at close range, and the sow charged. He couldn't remove the safety tab from the can in time to spray the bear.[12]

Whenever it's practical, carry your pepper spray in the same place all the time so you know exactly where to reach when there's a crisis. Most pepper spray comes with a nylon hip holster that has a Velcro flap top, and one manufacturer makes a cleverly designed holster that you can fire from a chest harness. Like a quick-draw artist in an old cowboy movie, you should practice releasing your pepper spray from the holster, drawing it to a firing position, and removing the safety tab. Practice again and again until it's automatic. It's easy to lose the little safety clip so you might want to tie a piece of elastic shock cord to it.

Most pepper spray manufacturers recommend that you test-fire every new can of pepper spray with a half-second burst. If your can of pepper spray has been sitting in the basement for a few months, you can do a makeshift pressure test by gently shaking the can. The contents won't slosh around noticeably if the pressure is good. If it feels like you're shaking a can of soup—if you can feel the liquid sloshing around with every shake—the can has probably lost pressure. In addition to checking the pressure, look for leakage from the seals, the actuator, and the edge of the canister. Incidentally, the AIBSEC says, "The best spray actuators are fire-extinguisher quality from Great Britain. The least reliable are from China."

A 1995 report on the use of pepper spray as a bear deterrent found that spraying curious brown bears approaching a camp stopped 20 out of 20 bears initially.[13] Two bears came back for a second look. In cases where brown bears charged or behaved in a threatening manner toward people, pepper spray initially stopped the bear's behavior 15 out of 16 times. Six of the sixteen bears continued to behave aggressively and three bears attacked the sprayers.

Pepper spray was less effective on black bears. When used on curious bears or bears looking for food and garbage, 19 out of 26 bears that were sprayed initially stopped what they were doing. Only 14 out of 26 bears left the area, and 6 of those 14 bears returned. When people sprayed black bears during sudden encounters or possible predatory situations, 4 out of 4 bears initially stopped their behavior. However, the bears did not leave the area in response to being sprayed.

These are all real-life incidents, not controlled tests in a lab. The results of the study are based on a total of 66 verifiable incidents, and the authors of the study caution that this is an extremely small sample size.

Larry Clark, from the Monell Chemical Senses Center, notes that Capsaicin may be effective only on the first hit. If a bear gets a good dose, leaves, and then returns a few minutes later, a second dose might not have much effect. Once saturated, the bear might not feel any pain no matter how much you spray it.[14]

Does Pepper Spray Attract Bears?

The purpose of bear pepper spray is to drive away a bear, and, if you use it properly—if you spray a full-power blast at a nearby bear—pepper spray has a high success rate. In BYU professor Tom Smith's database on pepper spray use in Alaska, there are 40 cases when people sprayed charging bears. "In 84 percent of those instances," he said, "the bear turned away."[15]

Pepper spray is often described as bear repellent, and perhaps this is what gave some people the idea they could spray it on their tent like mosquito repellent to keep bears away. Wrong. I saw this myself when I was living in Alaska. Bears occasionally clamber aboard float planes and cause damage, so one evening a pilot I knew sprayed his floats to keep bears away. The next morning there were deep bite marks in the aluminum floats.

Tom Smith actually got to see the bears in action. In 1997, Smith briefly sprayed a gravel bar on the Kulik River in Katmai National Park. The area was heavily used by brown bears. They loved the residue from the pepper spray. They rolled around on it. They leaned down and

For most people, pepper spray is more effective than a firearm.

rubbed their head and necks on it. The stuff was like catnip for bears. Smith videotaped the action. The hunting fraternity and other people who were skeptical about the stopping power of pepper spray were delighted that it attracted bears.

Which misses the point entirely. Pepper spray can attract bears if you don't use it properly—so use it properly.

If you ever have to spray a bear while you're out on an overnight trip, be aware that the spray residue on the can might attract bears. Wipe it clean with soap and water, and then store the empty can with your food and garbage. If you spray a bear entering your camp, you'd be wise to move your camp, even if you succeeded in driving away the bear.

FIREARMS OR PEPPER SPRAY?

In 1999, the U.S. Fish & Wildlife Service (FWS) sent out a press release with telling statistics from the Yellowstone region on the firearms vs. pepper spray debate. In Yellowstone Park, where firearms are forbidden, thousands of hikers rely on pepper spray for protection from bears. Meanwhile, on National Forest Service land adjacent to the park, thousands of hunters guided by commercial outfitters rely on firearms for protection from bears.

How does each group fare? According to the U.S. Fish and Wildlife Service, people in the Yellowstone region who encountered bears and defended themselves with "firearms suffer injury about 50% of the time ...persons defending themselves with pepper spray escaped injury over 90% of the time, and the remaining 5 to 10% experienced shorter duration attacks and less severe injuries."

Statistics from Tom Smith's database on Alaska bear attacks "show that 92 percent of people who used spray successfully deterred an aggressive or menacing bear. Firearms have performed less successfully when used to deter bear attacks—68 percent."[16]

I believe the main reason firearms have a low success rate against grizzlies is not the weapons, but the person handling the weapon—few hunters are competent at combat shooting, and trying to kill a grizzly that's charging toward you at 30 to 35 mph is definitely combat shooting. It's much easier for a novice to 'hit" and stop a grizzly bear with a cloud of pepper spray than it is for a novice to hit and stop a grizzly with a bullet the diameter of a pencil.

The most important tip I can pass along to help people use firearms or pepper spray more effectively is to practice firing quickly. Practice until it's instinctive. Practice until you can do it in the dark. Most dangerous encounters with grizzlies happen at close range and they're over in a heartbeat. If you don't practice using your firearm or pepper spray, you might find yourself staring in terror at a charging grizzly bear that's 30 yards away and roaring closer while you fumble around with your rifle, shotgun, pistol, or pepper spray.

In 1984, a man doing grizzly bear research in Yellowstone Park became something of a pepper spray poster boy when he foiled an attack with pepper spray. He first sprayed the grizzly at a distance of 20 feet and then again at 6 feet. After the bear knocked him down, he sprayed it directly in the face and it left. In articles about pepper spray, several national publications have used this incident to make the point that pepper spray really works.[17]

I'm not sure I agree one hundred percent with that conclusion. The researcher involved in this incident was working for the Interagency Grizzly Bear Study's "Bear Disturbance Crew," which was more commonly known as the "suicide squad." Their job was to go into backcountry areas and disturb bears to show how they reacted. This brings me to a point I can't emphasize strongly enough: Just because you have a can of pepper spray, don't go places you wouldn't go otherwise. Don't do things you wouldn't do otherwise. Try to guard against overconfidence. The record clearly shows that pepper spray can be effective for stopping bear attacks and even more so against curious or food-seeking bears. What the record doesn't tell us is how often the overconfidence fostered by pepper spray indirectly caused the same attacks.

In a book that's been dismissed as an infomercial for bear pepper spray (*True Stories of Bear Attacks: Who Survived and Why*) author Mike Lapinski tells tale after tale of people who see a bear or come across fresh bear sign, but keep going and have a confrontation with a bear. Sometimes pepper spray saves them from injury, but just as often they do get injured. Would people in the same situation turn around, or make noise and use other common sense precautions to avoid a confrontation if they didn't have pepper spray?

In a phone conversation, Yellowstone Grizzly Foundation Co-Director Steve French told me he's gone through three distinct phases on pepper spray. At first he categorically rejected it. Then he carried it everywhere and found that it made him too cocky. He couldn't control the overconfidence factor. Now he doesn't take pepper spray with him on day-to-day field excursions, but he does keep it handy in camp. French, an articulate man who describes himself as "the son of a Texas truck driver who happens to be a doctor," always reminds people that pepper spray "ain't brains in a can."

Epilogue

It just seems that cutting-edge science takes a decade or two to filter out and become common knowledge; meanwhile, old notions die slowly—especially, it seems, when it comes to bears.
Nick Jans, *The Grizzly Maze: Timothy Treadwell's Fatal Obsession with Alaskan Bears* (2005)

Slowly, way too slowly for me, old wives' tales about bears are fading away and being replaced by sound information from biologists. It's an uphill battle. For every obscure video like *Staying Safe in Bear Country*, there's a Hollywood movie like *The Edge*, and a popular documentary like Werner Herzog's *Grizzly Man*. For every fantastic book like *Living with Bears*, there are four dreadful books like *Shooting Bears: The Adventures of a Wildlife Photographer*. Stephen Herrero publishes "Human Injuries Inflicted By Bears In Alberta:1960–98" in a scientific journal with a circulation of 700; *Newsweek* and *Backpacker* publish off-the-wall articles about bear attacks.

In most cases, the errors and prejudicial remarks about bears are accidental. When I read books like *Bear vs. Man* or *Mark of the Grizzly*, there's no doubt in my mind the author's heart was in the right place—they're pro-bear, and they sincerely want to help bears and people co-exist—but there are so many egregious mistakes that the books are toxic.

I don't mean to sound pessimistic; I'm confident that in a decade or two, clichés about unpredictable bears having poor vision will be passé. Stripping away these illusions reveals the real bear. People can live with real bears; it's the bears roaming the wilds of the human imagination that are impossible to get along with. One positive trend I see today is that some books and videos help people see bear-human encounters from the bear's perspective. I'm not talking about goopy Disneyland anthropomorphism. People now realize that if you plant apple trees on your four-acre ranchette in Colorado, bears are going to climb your fence, help themselves to your apples, and say "thanks" by leaving behind a runny pile of bear scat. People now know that bears don't behave this way because they're "devilish;" they do it because they need all the calories they can get to survive a winter in hibernation. Knowledge fosters tolerance.

But we don't just tolerate bears; we're mystified by them. One June day a few years ago, I took an 11-mile hike to a fire lookout in Yellowstone Park. My friend Jim McBride set out a few hours behind me. I traveled through an open valley for the first 8 miles, and then started climbing up the timbered slopes of a mountain. The valley was snow-free, but there was snow on the mountain. I reached the top, took the shutters off the lookout, and made myself comfortable. When McBride arrived, he told me that about a mile up into the timber, he saw tracks coming out of the trees. Grizzly tracks. The bear followed me almost to the top of the mountain. Was it curious? Was it thinking of dining on me? Was it just going to the other side of the mountain?

Notes

INTRODUCTION

1 Alfred Runte, Yosemite: The Embattled Wilderness (Lincoln: University of Nebraska Press, 1990).

2 Alan Carey, "The Charge," Field & Stream, February 1984, 70.

3 North American Bear Center, *www.bear.org/Kids/Sounds.html*

CHAPTER 1: PLANNING A TRIP INTO BEAR COUNTRY

1 Terry DeBruyn, *Walking with Bears* (New York: The Lyons Press, 1999), 257.

2 Craig Medred, "Grizzly Sow, Cubs Surprise Two Hikers," *Anchorage Daily News,* October 28, 1997; "Bear Slashes Mountaineer," *Anchorage Daily News,* August 23, 1998.

3 Craig Medred, "Portable Electric Fences Are Bear Barriers," *Anchorage Daily News,* October 30, 2005.

4 Vin T. Sparano, "King of the Hill," *Outdoor Life,* June/July 1998, 101.

5 Jim Shockey, "Nightmare Bear," *North American Hunter,* December/January 2005, 36–40.

6 Scott McMillion, *Mark of the Grizzly* (Helena, MT: Falcon Press, 1998), 132.

7 Brad Garfield, *Bear Vs. Man: Recent Attacks and How to Avoid the Increasing Danger* (Minoqua, WI: Willow Creek Press, 2001), 13.

8 Safety in Bear Country Society/International Association for Bear Research and Management, *Staying Safe in Bear Country,* 2001, video/dvd.

9 J. Michael Kennedy and Christopher Reynolds, "Can We Get Along?" *Los Angeles Times,* October 1, 2003.

10 Stephen Herrero and Andrew Higgins, "Human–Black Bear Interactions," *Proceedings of the 5th Western Black Bear Workshop*, ed. Janene Auger and Hal L. Black (Provo, Utah, 1995).

11 Stephen Herrero, *Bear Attacks: Their Causes and Avoidance* (Guilford, CT: The Lyons Press, 2002), 105.

[12] McMillion, *Mark of the Grizzly,* 159.
[13] Alaska Interagency Bear Safety Education Committee (AIBSEC) Workshop Notes, March 23–24, 2000.

CHAPTER 2: BEAR EVOLUTION, BIOLOGY, AND BEHAVIOR

[1] AIBSEC Workshop Notes, March 23–24, 2000.
[2] Tom Smith, Stephen Herrero, and Steven C. Amstrup, "*The Bear That Never Was,*" *Alaska Magazine,* Sept. 2005, 22–27, 6.
[3] Stephen Herrero. 1978. A comparison of Some Features of the Evolution, Ecology and Behavior of Black and Grizzly/Brown bears, *Carnivore* 1(1):7–17.
[4] International Association for Bear Research and Management, *www.bearbiology.com/StayingSafeScript.htm*
[5] *Yellowstone Grizzly Journal* 8, no. 3 (Spring 1996).
[6] DeBruyn, *Walking with Bears,* 76.
[7] Sivik, J.G and D.J. Piggins. 1975. "Refractive State of the Eye of the Polar Bear (*Thalarctos maritimus*)," *Norwegian J. Zool.* 23(1) 89–91.
[8] Charles C. Schwartz, Sterling D. Miller, and Mark A. Haroldson *Wild Mammals of North America* (Baltimore: Johns Hopkins University Press, 2003), 562.
[9] DeBruyn, *Walking with Bears,* 51–52.
[10] Craig Medred, "Making Book on Bears," *Anchorage Daily News,* May 25, 1997.
[11] Riley Woodford, "Eyes of the Bear: Bears See Well, but Trust Noses More," *Alaska Wildlife News,* Alaska Department of Fish & Game, April, 2005.
[12] Cited in Ellis Sutton Bacon, "Investigation of Perception and Behavior of the American Black Bear (Ursus americanus)" (doctoral dissertation, University of Tennessee, Knoxville, 1973). The original report is by E. Kuckuk, "Tierpsychologische Beobachtungen an zwei jungen braunbaren," *Zeitschrift für Vergleichende Physiologie* 24 (1937): 14–41.
[13] Lyle Willmarth quoted by Tom Beck, letter to author, August 16, 1996.
[14] Woodford, *Alaska Wildlife News, April 2005.*
[15] Smith, Armstrup, and Herrero, "The Bear that Never Was," *Alaska Magazine,* Sept, 2005.
[16] Stringham, Stephen, Ph.D. *Beauty Within the Beast: Kinship With Bears in the Alaska Wilderness.* (Falls Village, CT: Lost Post Press, 2002), 167.
[17] Chris Peterson, *Hungry Horse News,* August 3, 2005.

[18]   Caroline Fraser, "You Are in Bear Country," *Outside Magazine,* March, 2001, 24.

[19]   Jeff Rennicke, *Bears of Alaska in Life and Legend* (Boulder, CO: Robert Rhinehart Publishing, 1987), 41; Richard R. Knight, Interagency Grizzly Bear Study Team Leader, personal correspondence, Feb. 29, 1996.

[20]   National Audubon Society and TBS, coproducers, *Grizzly and Man: Uneasy Truce,* 1989, video.

[21]   BearSmart Durango, *www.bearsmartdurango.org/qna.shtml.*

[22]   AIBSEC Workshop Notes, March 23–24, 2000.

[23]   Linda Masterson, *Living with Bears* (Masonville, CO: PixyJack Press, 2006), 39.

[24]   Tom Walker and Larry Aumiller, *River of Bears* (Stillwater, WY, Voyaguer Press, 1993), 40.

[25]   North American Bear Center, *www.bear.org/Kids/Sounds.html*

[26]   Derek Stonorov, letter to author, June 1996; Derek Stonorov and Allen W. Stokes, "Social Behavior of the Alaska Brown Bear," *Bears—Their Biology and Management,* n.s., no. 23 (Morges, Switzerland: International Union for the Conservation of Nature and Natural Resources, 1972), 232–42.

CHAPTER 3: MENSTRUATION, SEX, AND BEARS

[1]   E. Watson, "Grizzlies," *Sports Illustrated* 27, no. 19 (1967): 63–67.

[2]   "Smelly Socks Attract Grizzly," *Anchorage Daily News,* October 27, 1995.

[3]   Caroline P. Byrd, "Of Bears and Women: Investigating the Hypothesis that Menstruation Attracts Bears" (master's thesis, University of Montana, Missoula, 1988); U.S. Department of the Interior, National Park Service, *Glacier National Park, Grizzly Bear Attacks at Granite Park and Trout Lake in Glacier National Park,* August 13, 1967 (West Glacier, MT, 1967).

[4]   U.S. Department of the Interior, *Grizzly Bear Attacks,* 21–22.

[5]   Bruce S. Cushing, "The Effects of Human Menstrual Odors, Other Scents, and Ringed Seal Vocalizations on the Polar Bear" (master's thesis, University of Montana, Missoula, 1980).

[6]   C. R. Morey, wilderness specialist, to administrative officer, memorandum, "Backcountry Assignments for Female Employees," November 13, 1980, Glacier National Park.

[7]   B. Blacker, L. Tryon, G. Johnson, K. Ahlenslager, L. Williams, M. Eisheid, G. Seeley, P. Lazo, and S. Gill, to acting superintendent, letter, December 15, 1980, Glacier National Park.

8   Hutchison, acting regional director, to regional director, Rocky Mountain Region, memorandum, *Backcountry Assignments for Female Employees,* May 29, 1981.

9   Jean O'Neil, acting superintendent, Glacier National Park, management directive no. 203.4, *Women in the Backcountry,* April 6, 1984.

10 Stephen Herrero, *Bear Attacks,* 139.

11 Lynn L. Rogers and S. S. Scott, "Reactions of Black Bears to Human Menstrual Odors," *Journal of Wildlife Management* 55, no. 4 (1991): 632–34.

12 Kerry A. Gunther, "Bears and Menstruating Women," Yellowstone National Park, Information Paper BMO-7, 1995.

13 Walker and Aumiller, *River of Bears,* 131.

14 Byrd, "Of Bears and Women."

CHAPTER 4: COOKING AND FOOD STORAGE

1   Bill Schneider, *Bear Aware* (Guilford, CT: Falcon Press, 2004), 19.

2   William B. Cella and Jeffery A. Keay, *Annual Bear Management and Incident Report* (National Park Service, Yosemite National Park, 1980).

3   Herrero, *Bear Attacks,* 121.

4   Craig Medred, "Making Book on Bears."

5   Kerry Gunther, personal communication, November 1996.

6   Associated Press, "Young Grizzly Killed After Being Fed," May 23, 2003.

7   Steve and Marilyn French, "The Predatory Behavior of Grizzly Bears Feeding on Elk Calves in Yellowstone National Park, 1986–1988," study presented at the International Conference on Bear Research and Management, 1990.

CHAPTER 5: CAMPING AND TRAVEL TIPS

1   Schneider, *Bear Aware,* 27.

2   *Backpacker Magazine,* October, 1990.

3   Peterson, David. "The 'Blend In' Theory," *Backpacker,* October, 2000.

4   Chris Batin, "Bear Attacks!" *Outdoor Life,* August, 2003, 48.

5   Kerry Gunther and Hopi Hoekstra, "Bear-Inflicted Human Injuries in Yellowstone, 1980–1994," *Yellowstone Science 4,* no. 1 (Winter, 1996): 2–9.

6   Safety in Bear Country Society/International Association for Bear Research and Management, *Staying Safe in Bear Country,* 2001, video/dvd.

[7] Stephen Herrero, *Bear Attacks,* xii.

[8] Tom Beck, *Hunting & Shooting Sports Education Journal 3,* vol. 1 (Summer, 2003)

[9] Craig Medred, "Safety-Conscious Travel Helps Bear Country Trekkers Avoid the Danger Zone," *Anchorage Daily News,* May 15, 2005.

[10] Chuck Neal, *Grizzlies in the Mist* (Moose, WY & San Francisco: Homestead Publishing, 2003), 72–73.

[11] Steven P. French, M.D., section in "Bites and Injuries Inflicted by Mammals," *Management of Wilderness and Environmental Emergencies,* 3rd ed., ed. Paul S. Aeuerbach (St. Louis: C. V. Mosby, 1995).

[12] DeBruyn, *Walking with Bears,* 64.

[13] Schneider, *Bear Aware,* 69–70.

[14] Tom Beck in *Buffalo News,* July 19,1999.

[15] Stringham, *Beauty Within the Beast,* 3–4.

[16] Stephen Herrero, *Proceedings of the 5th Western Black Bear Workshop.*

[17] Kathy Etling, "Staring Death in the Face, Bear Attacks of 1998," *Bears and Other Top Predators,* Vol.1, Issue 1; 9, 7–10.

[18] Peter Porco, "Hunting Guide mauled by Wounded Brown Bear," *Anchorage Daily News,* April 28, 2004.

[19] Steve French, telephone conversation with author, September 1996.

[20] McMillion, *Mark of the Grizzly,* 159.

[21] Jerry Lewanski, quoted in "Bear Attacks Force Alaska Joggers to Find Safe Ways to Exercise," *Christian Science Monitor,* September 6, 1995.

CHAPTER 6: BEARS AND HUMAN RECREATION

[1] Erwin Bauer, "Big Bears," *Outdoor Photographer,* March 1996, 40–43, 104–5.

[2] Brad Garfield, *Bear vs. Man: Recent Attacks and How to Avoid the Increasing Danger* (Minoqua, WI: Willow Creek Press, 2001), 188; Alan Carey, *In the Path of the Grizzly,* (Flagstaff, AZ: Northland Publishing, 1986) p.12–14; Erwin Bauer, "Big Bears," *Outdoor Photographer,* March 1996, 40–43, 104–5; Stephen Herrero, *Bear Attacks: Their Causes and Avoidance,* 31.

[3] Jim Mann, "Grizzly Man," *Kalispell Daily Inter Lake,* April 1, 2005.

[4] Tom Smith, personal email to author, 2006.

[5] Tom Smith quoted by Chris Batin in "Bears in Mind," *Western Outdoors,* October 2004, 36.

6   Bill Sherwonit, "Where the Wild Things Remain," *National Parks and Conservation Association*, Spring, 2004.
7   Scott McMillion, *Mark of the Grizzly*, 94.
8   Tom Stienstra, "Some Basic Truths of Mountain Biking," *San Francisco Examiner*, 1996. Reprint, *Anchorage Daily News*, September 1, 1996.
9   Angus M. Thuemer Jr., *Jackson Hole News & Guide*, September 4, 2004.
10 U.S. Fish and Wildlife Service, Wyoming Department of Fish and Game, Interagency Grizzly Bear Committee, "Mountain Biking," brochure (No photographer, no date).
11 Harvey Manning, quoted by Peter Potterfield, in "The Warrior Writer," *Backpacker*, August 1996, 56–62.
12 National Park Service, Grant Teton National Park, News Release, March 8, 2001.
13 *Yellowstone Center for Resources 2000 Annual Report*
14 *Helena Independent Reporter* staff, "Warm January Brings Bear out of Den," February 18, 2006

CHAPTER 7: CLOSE ENCOUNTERS

1   Masterson, *Living with Bears*, 208.
2   Neal, *Grizzlies in the Mist*, 120–1.
3   Larry Aumiller, letter to author, June 1996.
4   Chris Batin, "Fishing in Bear Country," *Fairbanks News Miner*, July 18, 2003.
5   Brad Garfield, *Bear vs. Man: Recent Attacks and How to Avoid the Increasing Danger* (Minoqua, WI: Willow Creek Press, 2001), 85.
6   AIBSEC, p.5
7   Larry Aumiller, letter to author, June 1996.
8   Polly Hessing, letter to author, June 30, 1996.
9   DeBruyn, *Walking with Bears*, 159.
10 Benjamin Kilham and Ed Gray, *Among the Bears*, (New York: Holt, 2002), 223.
11 Stringham, *Beauty Within the Beast*, 123.
12 James Gary Shelton, *Bear Attacks: The Deadly Truth* (Hagensborg, British Columbia: Pallister Publishing, 1998), 88–89.
13 Herrero, *Bear Attacks: Their Causes and Avoidance*, 105.
14 Shelton, *Bear Attacks: The Deadly Truth*, 13.
15 *Cleveland Plain Dealer*, October 1, 2000
16 Shelton, *Bear Attacks II: Myth and Reality* (Hagensborg, British Columbia: Pallister Publishing, 1998), 20.

[17] Mark Freeman, "Bear Attacks Prompt Look at Self-Defense Law," *Medford Mail Tribune*, May 27, 2001.

[18] Zaz Hollander and Craig Medred, "Hungry-Looking Black Bear Gives Hiker a Scare," *Anchorage Daily News,* August 16, 2002.

[19] Natalie St. Denis, "Safety Tips in Bear Country," *Canadian Geographic,* January 2002.

[20] Mike Lapinski, True Stories of *Bear Attacks: Who Survived and Why* (Portland, OR: Graphic Arts Center Publishing Company, 2004).

[21] Stephen Herrero and Andrew Higgins, "Human Injuries Inflicted by Black Bears in British Columbia: 1960–97.,"*Ursus* 11, 209–218.

[22] Craig Medred, "In Bear Country, You Just Can't Be too Careful," *Anchorage Daily News*, July 17, 2005.

[23] Smith, Armstrup, and Herrero, "The Bear that Never Was," *Alaska Magazine,* Sept, 2005.

[24] Steve French, "Bear Attacks." This is the draft version of French's section that later appeared in *Auerbach, Management of Wilderness and Environmental Emergencies.*

[25] Stringham, *Beauty Within the Beast,* 89.

[26] U.S. Department of the Interior, National Park Service, "The Bears Are Not to Blame," brochure (Washington, D.C., 1995); Steve Thompson, Yosemite's Resource Management Office, telephone conversation with author, September 1996.

[27] McMillion, *Mark of the Grizzly*, 64.

[28] Terry DeBruyn, *Walking with Bears*, 11.

[29] French, "Bear Attacks."

CHAPTER 8: GUNS AND PEPPER SPRAY

[1] U.S. Department of the Interior, Fish and Wildlife Service in Alaska, Revised Region 7, memorandum QIPC, *Bear Safety Policies*, August 2, 1995; Department of Renewable Resources, Government of the Northwest Territories, *Safety in Bear Country,* rev. ed. (Yellowknife, 1992).

[2] John Stevens, Wrangell Ranger District, Tongass National Forest, phone conversation with author, October 1996.

[3] Hod Coburn, email to the author, July 8, 2002.

[4] Mike Crammod, *Of Bears and Men* (Norman, OK: University of Oklahoma, 1986), 117.

[5] Peter Porco, "Hunting Guide Mauled by Wounded Brown Bear," *Anchorage Daily News*, April 28, 2004; Jeff Cooper, "Thoughts from the Gunner's Guru," *Guns & Ammo*, February 2006, 80.

[6] "Playing Back a Bear Attack," *Anchorage Daily News,* October 4, 1992.

[7] Scott McMillion, *Mark of the Grizzly,* 141–153.

8   Craig Medred, "Bear Country Need Not Be a Death Trap for Runners," *Anchorage Daily* News, June 11, 2006.

9   Herrero, *Bear Attacks,* 73.

10 McMillion, *Mark of the Grizzly*, 136.

11 Michael Jamison, "Bear attacks, injures hiker in Glacier Park," *Missoulian*, August 15, 2000.

12 Scott McMillion, "Lone Hiker Never Had a Chance Against Grizzly," *Bozeman Daily Chronicle*, September 24, 1999.

13 Stephen Herrero and Andrew Higgins, "Field Use of Capsaicin Sprays as a Bear Deterrent," in *Proceedings, 10th International Conference on Bear Research and Management* (Fairbanks: IUCN Bear Specialists Group, 1995).

14 Craig Medred, "Pepper Spray? Bad Bet," *Anchorage Daily News,* October 6, 1996.

15 Craig Medred, "Safety-Conscious Travel Helps Bear Country Trekkers Avoid the Danger Zone" *Anchorage Daily News*, May 15, 2005.

16 Smith, *The Bear that Never Was*

17 Gary Turbak, "A Defensive Solution: When Bear Meets Man, a Spray Derived from Red Peppers May Save the Day," *Field & Stream,* June 1987, 59, 109–10.

PHOTO CREDITS

ILLUSTRATION CREDITS

Recommended References

BOOKS

Beecham, John J., and Jeff Rohlman. *A Shadow in the Forest: Idaho's Black Bear.* Boise: Idaho Department of Fish and Game; Moscow: University of Idaho Press, 1994. Although the writing is a bit dry and academic, the facts are exciting. This is essential reading for conservationists.

DeBruyn, Terry D. *Walking with Bears: One Man's Relationship with Three Generations of Wild Bears.* 1999. Guilford, CT: Lyons Press. Detailed information about black bears by a biologist who spent six years in close contact with bear families in Michigan.

Fair, Jeff. *The Great American Bear.* Minoqua, WI: NorthWord Press, 1990. Covers basic black bear biology as well as bear conservation efforts and bear–human interactions. It's accurate and easy to read.

Lynch, Wayne. *Bears: Monarchs of the Northern Wilderness.* Seattle, WA: Mountaineers Books, 1993. If you want just one book that gives in-depth coverage about the biology and ecology of black bears, grizzly bears, and polar bears, this is it.

Masterson, Linda. *Living with Bears: A Practical Guide to Bear Country.* Foreword and technical editing by Tom Beck. Masonville, CO: PixyJack Press, 2006. This long overdue book gives expert advice on coping with bears in typical rural and suburban settings: the bear after your birdfeeder or your apple trees. It prepares you for the bears you might meet at a small U.S. Forest Service campground on a dirt road way back in the woods. It has great tips for sportsmen. The writing is wonderful; it's fun to read. Thanks to Beck's editing, it's accurate. This is far and away the most useful book ever written about bears.

Neal, Chuck. *Grizzlies in the Mist.* Moose, WY: Homestead Publishing, 2003. This accurate, educational, and entertaining book about grizzlies in the Yellowstone region was written by an ecologist who spent years observing bears without disturbing them.

Peacock, Doug. *Grizzly Year.* New York: Henry Holt and Company, 1990. Native Americans called grizzlies the "medicine bear." This is a real-life story of how the medicine bear heals the spiritual wounds of a Vietnam vet. Bear biology, wilderness philosophy, and wonderful writing.

Rogers, Lynn. "Watchable Wildlife: The Black Bear," 1992. North Central Distribution Center, One Gifford Pinchot Drive, Madison, WI 53705-2398. This U.S. Forest Service brochure provides a great capsule summary (eighteen pages) about black bears and how to get along with them.

Shepard, Paul, and Barry Sanders. *The Sacred Paw: The Bear in Nature, Myth, and Literature.* New York: Viking Penguin, 1985. Even if the closest you've ever been to a bear is eating a bear claw pastry from a bakery, this book shows how deeply bears are ingrained in our conscious and subconscious minds.

Snyder, Susan. *Bear in Mind: The California Grizzly.* Berkeley: Heydey Books, 2003. I'd buy this book for the remarkable illustrations alone. Snyder is the head of Access Service at the University of California's Bancroft Library, and she's included everything from 19th century paintings of Grizzly Adams to teddy bear cartoons to an 1865 photo of a "grizzly bear chair." The text tells the history of grizzlies and people in California. What makes it unique is that Snyder dug up hundreds of lengthy quotes and passages from books, newspapers and other sources. It's kind of a living history because, in their own words, people from the 1600s–1900s reveal the attitude of the day toward bears. Each chapter opens with thoughtful introductory remarks by Snyder, and her writing is quite graceful.

Stonorov, Derek. **Living in Harmony with Bears,** (Homer, AK: National Audubon Society, 2000). This exceptional booklet was written by one of the world's leading authorities on brown bear behavior. Stonorov gives clear, concise advice on how to avoid trouble with bears, and how to handle dangerous encounters. He does an outstanding job of helping people understand the motivations of bears. Practical information for hikers, homeowners, hunters, and fishermen. Available for online purchase from the Alaska National History Association (*www.alaskanha.org*).

Stringham, Stephen, Ph.D. *Beauty Within the Beast: Kinship With Bears in the Alaska Wilderness.* Falls Village, CT: Lost Post Press, 2002. Stringham raised three orphaned black bear cubs. It's a good story; as you can imagine, the bear family—and Stringham was definitely part of the family—had adventures and misadventures. But what makes this book valuable is that Stringham provides a treasure trove of information about black bear behavior. Excellent.

Walker, Tom. *River of Bears*. Stillwater, MN: Voyageur Press, 1993. A special book about a special place—Alaska's McNeil River—that offers an enlightened view of bears.

VIDEOS

On the Trail of Pennsylvania's Black Bears. Pennsylvania Game Commission, 2001 Elmerten Avenue, Harrisburg, PA 17110-9797; (717) 787-7015. Provides comprehensive coverage about the behavior, biology, and habits of black bears.

Staying Safe in Bear Country: A Behavioral-Based Approach to Reducing Risk, distributed by the *IBA* (*www.bearbiology.com*) and Distribution Access (*www.distribution access.com*) (888)-440 4640. This outstanding video was produced by Alaska Department of Fish and Game biologist John Hechtel with assistance from the *IBA's* Safety in Bear Country Society. Remarkable footage of bears interacting with people. Stephen Herrero and many of North America's top bear safety experts contributed to this video.

Way of the [Brown] Bear in Alaska. Distributed by Bullfrog Films, P.O. Box 149, Oley, PA 19547; 1-800-543-3764, (*www.bullfrogfilms.com*). Focuses entirely on bear behavior.

WEBSITES

Most websites are marred by inaccurate, prejudicial information about bears, and some websites include truly dangerous advice. Here are two websites I trust:

Yellowstone Grizzly Foundation (*www.yellowstonegrizzly.com*). At this site you'll find fascinating facts about grizzlies in the Yellowstone region, and detailed information on bear attacks.

Ph.D wildlife biologist Thomas S. Smith (*www.absc.usgs.gov/staff/MFEB/tsmith.php*). Tom Smith (no relation) is doing practical research in Alaska that benefits outdoors people in bear country: how effective are bear bells, does pepper spray attract bears under certain circumstances, and more. You'll find various bear-related topics to explore here, including pragmatic safety tips and detailed statistics on bear attacks.

Index

About the Author

Dave Smith is a naturalist who has worked in Yellowstone, Glacier, Glacier Bay, and Denali National Parks, and as a fire lookout in northwest Montana for three summers. Dave's outdoor adventures have included a solo canoe trip from Yellowstone National Park to the Missouri River in North Dakota and a forty-day stay in the remote, rarely visited desert canyons in central Arizona.

Dave lectures widely on bears and has appeared with Jack Hanna in a documentary on Glacier Bay National Park aired by PBS and The Nature Channel. He is the author of *Alaska's Mammals*, and *Don't Get Eaten*. He resides in Bisbee, Arizona.

THE MOUNTAINEERS, founded in 1906, is a nonprofit outdoor activity and conservation club, whose mission is "to explore, study, preserve, and enjoy the natural beauty of the outdoors ...." Based in Seattle, Washington, the club is now the third-largest such organization in the United States, with seven branches throughout Washington State.

The Mountaineers sponsors both classes and year-round outdoor activities in the Pacific Northwest, which include hiking, mountain climbing, ski-touring, snowshoeing, bicycling, camping, kayaking, nature study, sailing, and adventure travel. The club's conservation division supports environmental causes through educational activities, sponsoring legislation, and presenting informational programs.

All club activities are led by skilled, experienced instructors who are dedicated to promoting safe and responsible enjoyment and preservation of the outdoors.

If you would like to participate in these organized outdoor activities or the club's programs, consider a membership in The Mountaineers. For information and an application, write or call The Mountaineers, Club Headquarters, 300 Third Avenue West, Seattle, WA 98119; 206-284-6310. You can also visit the club's website at *www.mountaineers.org* or contact The Mountaineers via email at *clubmail@mountaineers.org.*

The Mountaineers Books, an active, nonprofit publishing program of the club, produces guidebooks, instructional texts, historical works, natural history guides, and works on environmental conservation. All books produced by The Mountaineers Books fulfill the club's mission.

Send or call for our catalog of more than 500 outdoor titles:

The Mountaineers Books
1001 SW Klickitat Way, Suite 201
Seattle, WA 98134
800-553-4453
mbooks@mountaineersbooks.org
www.mountaineersbooks.org

The Mountaineers Books is proud to be a corporate sponsor of The Leave No Trace Center for Outdoor Ethics, whose mission is to promote and inspire responsible outdoor recreation through education, research, and partnerships. The Leave No Trace program is focused specifically on human-powered (nonmotorized) recreation.

Leave No Trace strives to educate visitors about the nature of their recreational impacts, as well as offer techniques to prevent and minimize such impacts. Leave No Trace is best understood as an educational and ethical program, not as a set of rules and regulations.

For more information, visit *www.LNT.org,* or call 800-332-4100.

OTHER TITLES BY THE MOUNTAINEERS BOOKS

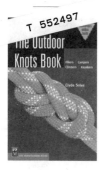

THE OUTDOOR KNOTS BOOK
Clyde Soles
A guide to the ropes and knots used
in the outdoors by hikers, campers,
paddlers, and climbers.

MOUNTAIN WEATHER: Backcountry
Forecasting & Weather Safety for
Hikers, Campers, Climbers,
Skiers, Snowboarders, *Jeff Renner*
Does the weather say "go"
or "stay home"?

WILDERNESS NAVIGATION: Finding
Your Way Using Map, Compass,
Altimeter, & GPS, 2nd Ed.
Bob & Mike Burns
Learn to navigate to anywhere,
from anywhere.

EVERYDAY WISDOM:
1001 EXPERT TIPS FOR
HIKERS, *Karen Berger*
Expert tips and tricks for hikers
and backpackers selected
from one of the most popular
Backpacker magazine columns.

BACKCOUNTRY COOKING: FROM
PACK TO PLACE IN 10 MINUTES
Dorcas Miller
Over 144 recipes and tips for
planning simple meals.

DON'T FORGET THE DUCT
TAPE: TIPS AND TRICKS FOR
REPAIRING
OUTDOOR GEAR
Kristin Hostetter

The Mountaineers Books has more than
500 outdoor recreation titles in print.
Receive a free catalog at
www.mountaineersbooks.org.